America's Voice in the Courts

The Washington Legal Foundation

by
Travis Ryan

Foreword by U.S. Senator Orrin Hatch

Copyright © 1991
Dogwood Press

ALL RIGHTS RESERVED

Library of Congress Catalog Card Number 91-072920

DEDICATION

This book is dedicated to all those honest, mainstream Americans for whom the Washington Legal Foundation is a powerful voice in our nation's courts and especially to those whose commitment and support make it possible for the Foundation to carry on its work.

TABLE OF CONTENTS

Foreword by U.S. Senator Orrin Hatch vii

A Voice for Victims 1

Keeping America Free—And Strong 15

Lawyer for the Little Guy 31

Protecting the Civil Rights of *All* Americans 46

Fighting the War Against Drugs 59

What Side of the Drug War Are These
    Judges On? 66

Judges Need to Be Reminded of Role in America's
    Justice System 74

Time to Bar the Bar Association 88

Battling Back: A New Weapon in the War 98

FOREWORD

There's no other group in the country like it.

There are more visible and vocal groups. There are bigger groups. There are groups with a lot more money.

In fact, there are over 150 so-called public interest groups pushing an antibusiness, procriminal agenda in America's courts—and in the media.

The ACLU alone outnumbers WLF's lawyers by a 15 to 1 ratio.

Yet, America has no more effective voice in the courts or in the regulatory arena than the Washington Legal Foundation.

WLF has played a leading role in public interest law for 14 years. During that time, this dedicated group of lawyers has increased its practical impact on the judiciary and on other legal policymakers, all the while deepening its commitment to the principles on which it was founded: economic and individual rights, civil liberties for business people, due process for the victims of violent crime, a strong national defense, and limited and accountable government.

Until WLF, "public interest" seemed to be synonymous with the term "liberal."

Groups like the ACLU, like Ralph Nader's Public Citizen group, like William Kunstler's Center for Constitutional Rights, had exerted enormous influence over America's court system and were the darlings of the news media.

WLF has changed all that.

For example, they were one of the first groups in America to take an activist role in the area of victims' rights. WLF believes, as most Americans do, that the rights of crime victims have been made secondary to the rights of those who commit those crimes. WLF also believes, as most Americans do, that this prioritization is wrong!

The foundation's skill at legal issues management has raised its public profile to an all-time high. Its professional staff produces high-quality work in a wide variety of landmark cases.

The result is that, when those other groups go into court today, they find themselves up against a most worthy adversary.

In the 1989–90 term alone, WLF was in the Supreme Court 15 times. In nine of those cases, they walked out on the winning side. America also walked out a winner.

There's every reason to believe that those cases could just as easily have gone the other way without WLF's involvement.

The national media quickly turn to WLF when they seek authoritative commentary on the most important issues of the day, because the foundation has become a respectable advocate of a reasonable judiciary.

In the process, WLF makes inroads each and every day by going toe-to-toe against activist lawyers in the courtroom, on radio and television, in print, and in the law schools—in every conceivable public forum.

WLF opposes the antibusiness views and the sometimes one-sided social goals of such well-funded groups as the ACLU, the NAACP Legal Defense Fund, Norman Lear's People for the American Way, the Sierra Club, and the Natural Resources Defense Council.

A list of WLF's well-known clients over the years reads like a who's who of conservative, mainstream America.

More than 250 U.S. Senators, U.S. Representatives, and state attorneys general have turned to WLF for help in precedent-setting cases all across the country.

WLF has sided with presidents and opposed presidents.

A list of their opponents over the years reads like a hall of liberal activism, including groups that frequently work against the principles that made this nation great.

WLF views its mission as serving as an effective counterweight to such liberal activists and offering a persuasive voice for reason and moderation. The foundation challenges our courts and regulatory agencies to make our legal system work for all Americans, not just for those on the ideological fringe of society, who are all too successful at passing off their own interests as the "public" interest.

Unlike many organizations that spend a great deal of time talking about what needs to be fixed in America, WLF spends its time fixing it.

Yet they accomplish all this without accepting court-awarded (taxpayer) fees or government grants, and without professional fund-raisers.

WLF has been my own voice in the courts on more than one occasion. I not only appreciate the assistance they have provided me, I admire them for their commitment, for their dedication, and for their aggressiveness in standing up and fighting for everything that is right about America.

A Voice for Victims

Washington Legal Foundation was one of the earliest and has remained among the most consistent loud and clear voices for the victims of crime.

Like most Americans, WLF's President and General Counsel Dan Popeo and others at WLF are fed up with a justice system that, over the past few decades, has put the rights of vicious, violent criminals far above the rights of their victims and above the rights of all decent, honest Americans.

So, since its founding, everyone at WLF has worked to right that wrong in every way possible, from blowing the whistle on ultralenient judges to battling for the application of the death penalty, from pushing for stiff mandatory uniform sentencing programs to removing the restrictions that make it next to impossible for America's law enforcement agencies to do their job effectively, and much more.

WLF was also one of the first groups to address the fact that one of the best ways to help the victims of crime is to make sure those victims get their day in court so that their voice is heard, too.

South Carolina v. Gathers

Like the voice of Richard Haynes' family.

Richard was a 32-year-old self-proclaimed preacher in South Carolina.

One day, as he sat on a bench in a city park with his usual assortment of such religious articles as Bibles, rosaries, statues, and prayer cards, Richard was confronted by a roving gang of thugs.

One of the members of that gang was a man named Demetrius Gathers.

Gathers and his pals decided to rob Richard. To make their job easier, they first beat him into unconsciousness, primarily through several blows to the head with a bottle.

Even after his fellow gang members left, however, Gathers, obviously enjoying himself immensely, stayed on and continued to batter the unconscious Richard, including inflicting a vicious, terrible sexual assault with an umbrella.

Then he went through Richard's bags to see if there was anything else to steal, throwing Richard's Bibles and other religious objects all around the park grounds.

He then left briefly, but returned with a knife. To make sure his work was complete, he stabbed this totally defenseless man.

At his trial, it didn't take a great deal of deliberation for the jury to return guilty verdicts for the crimes of murder and first degree sexual assault.

Nor did it take them long the following day to agree unanimously on the sentence: death by electrocution.

Richard's family, including his mother, the Rev. Dorothy Haynes, could at least feel that justice would be done.

But it would not be. At least not yet.

A year after his conviction and sentence, Demetrius Gathers' appeal reached the South Carolina Supreme Court, thanks to the usual pack of ultraliberal lawyers who have no regard either for the law or for the victims of violent crime.

In that state Supreme Court, the judges upheld

Gathers' conviction, but reversed the death sentence.

Their "reasoning?" That the closing remarks made to the jury by the prosecutor "conveyed the suggestion that [Gathers] deserved a death sentence because the victim was a religious man and a registered voter."

Those thoughtful jurists somehow decided that such a "suggestion" violated Demetrius Gathers' constitutional rights.

What about Richard Haynes' rights, or the rights of his family, of his mother who grieved so for the loss of her son?

When WLF got involved in this case, General Counsel Dan Popeo left no doubt about the reasons why:

> *It's sick and it's wrong when criminals have more rights than their victims and more than honest, mainstream Americans like you and me.*
>
> *Whether or not Richard Haynes was a religious person is not the issue here. Whether or not he was a registered voter is not the issue here.*
>
> *The issue here is pure and simple. Demetrius Gathers committed a brutal, vicious, animalistic assault on another human being and killed him.*
>
> *He deserves the death sentence the jury recommended.*

When *South Carolina v. Gathers* went before the Supreme Court, WLF was there representing not only Richard Haynes' mother but also the Crime Victims Legal Clinic; the Sunny Von Bulow National Victim Advocacy Center; Parents of Murdered Children; the Stephanie Roper Committee; the Unity Group, Inc.; and the State of New Mexico.

Unfortunately, the Court decided in a 5–4 decision to uphold the South Carolina Supreme Court decision to reverse Gathers' death sentence.

But, even as WLF's attorneys grieved with Mrs. Haynes over this miscarriage of justice, they also promised her they would be back, that they would not let her son's death be truly in vain.

Payne v. Tennessee

And, just before this book went to press, WLF *was* back in the Supreme Court, once again arguing for the right of victims' voices, including those of the victims' families, to be heard in court.

This time the murder victims were a young mother named Charisse Christopher and her infant daughter Lacie.

Pervis Tyrone Payne, in an incredibly brutal, vicious, cold-blooded assault, stabbed Charisse at least 50 times and stabbed tiny little Lacie repeatedly as well.

There was also a third victim of Payne's animalistic assault, Lacie's older brother, 3-year-old Nicholas.

Although he too was stabbed several times, including at least once in the neck, Nicky somehow survived his wounds.

Payne was convicted of the two murders and the attempted murder of little Nicholas.

At the sentencing phase of the trial, Mary Zvolanek, Nicky's grandmother, who took custody of him after the murders, testified about the effects of this brutal crime on Nicholas.

She simply told how he often cried for his mother and sister and could not understand why they did not come home.

At the conclusion of the sentencing hearing, the jury imposed a death sentence on Pervis Tyrone Payne.

Yet, as this was written, the U.S. Supreme Court had agreed to consider whether or not the introduction of Ms. Zvolanek's testimony into that sentencing hearing somehow violated Payne's constitutional rights.

As usual, the ACLU and a host of other liberal groups supporting Payne insist that it is such a violation—once again caring nothing about the rights of Nicholas, his slain mother and sister, or his grandmother.

They object to one person addressing the jury to talk about the impact this horrible crime has had on one of the victims, yet that same jury was subjected to a nonstop parade of people all testifying to the wonderful character of Pervis Tyrone Payne.

No wonder the American people are fed up with a justice system that is so heavily weighted in favor of the criminals with little or no recognition for those criminals' victims.

And it's not a matter of guilt or innocence. The Supreme Court is not reviewing Payne's conviction, only the death sentence he received.

WLF is asking the Supreme Court to take a major step toward righting the terrible wrong done to victims in this country, asking the Court to uphold Payne's death sentence and to overrule previous decisions (including *South Carolina v. Gathers*) which forbid the introduction of such victim impact evidence.

In addition to Nicky's grandparents, Joseph and Mary Zvolanek, WLF is representing the Stephanie Roper Committee, Parents of Murdered Children, the National Victim Center, People Against Child Abuse, Inc., and Parents & Friends of Missing Persons & Violent Crime Victims.

McCarthy, et al. v. Hinckley

One of Washington Legal Foundation's longest-running efforts on behalf of crime victims is a $14 million civil lawsuit filed against John W. Hinckley, Jr.

America stood in horror in March of 1981, waiting for word about the condition of President Ronald Reagan who had just been shot outside a Washington hotel by a lone gunman.

Not just the President fell to John Hinckley's bullets. There were even initial reports from the broadcast media that Presidential Press Secretary Jim Brady had been killed in the assassination attempt. Of course, as the nation well knows now, that report was false; and in one of the most remarkable, even miraculous, medical recoveries of all time, Jim Brady has returned to be as active, and certainly as visible, on the national scene as he ever was.

But another victim of Hinckley's bullets didn't stay in the headlines as much as Reagan and Brady—Presidential Secret Service Agent Timothy J. McCarthy.

Like every Agent attached to the Presidential

detail, McCarthy readily placed his own life in jeopardy to save the President of the United States. And it was in the course of carrying out his courageous actions that he was seriously wounded by Hinckley.

Yet the outrage was far from over. Even as a horrified nation was beginning to recover from the shock of the assassination attempt, a new sense of horror emerged when Americans found out that Hinckley would be found not guilty by reason of insanity.

However, WLF was determined not to let this case end there. Since 1981, the Foundation has been representing Agent McCarthy in that $14 million lawsuit for the damages he suffered in John Hinckley's assault. Jim Brady and a wounded police officer also filed suit.

It has been a long and convoluted struggle, with Hinckley's lawyers doing everything possible to derail the WLF effort.

But at each step of the way, WLF has won on critical issues: had psychiatric records unsealed for help in preparing the case, finally got permission to take depositions from Hinckley himself, and more.

And despite all the delays, the case is expected to go to trial in the summer of 1991 unless it is settled.

One of the more interesting side aspects of the case is that, during any trial, Hinckley would once again have to prove he was insane and, as the Foundation's Executive Legal Director Paul Kamenar noted, "A civil jury may not make the same ruling as the jury in the criminal case."

Kamenar also explained the reason for the Foundation's continuing pursuit of the case against Hinckley even though he seems to have no resources with which to pay damages of any kind.

Kamenar noted that in cases like this one, judgment can be given for any future assets, and the judgment period can be for as long as 20 years. Furthermore, that judgment period can be renewed.

"Even your rapist or mugger may win the D.C. lottery a year from now, and you can say, 'Sorry, pal, that money belongs to me.'"

Of course, in Hinckley's case the prospects of future assets are somewhat greater than the odds of winning the D.C. lottery.

At the first available opportunity, publishers and producers will be beating down his door with lucrative book and movie contracts.

When they do, WLF wants to be there to collect every penny possible and turn it over to Secret Service Agent Tim McCarthy.

Crime Doesn't Pay?

The ability of admitted, convicted criminals to profit from their illegal actions even after they've been thrown in jail was the focus of another WLF case, this one involving the giant publishing house, Simon & Schuster.

The case centered around an unholy alliance between that publishing company and a low-life mobster named Henry Hill—an admitted murder accomplice, drug dealer, and loan shark.

Simon & Schuster thought Hill's disgusting story would make good reading—and good profits—so they offered him an exorbitant sum for the rights to his story.

The result of that fat contract was *Wiseguy*, a best-seller written by Nicholas Pileggi and published in 1985.

Hill received more than $125,000 from Simon & Schuster, plus he earned a share of the over $500,000 paid for movie rights to his story.

The publisher was happy, the criminal was ecstatic. But there was one minor problem—it was all against the law.

A decade earlier, New York had passed a law (known as the "Son of Sam" law) to prevent that infamous serial killer, David Berkowitz, and other criminals from profiting through the sale of their stories for book or movie contracts. (Similar laws were subsequently passed in at least 41 other states and adopted by Congress as well.)

Invoking that law, New York State ordered Henry Hill to turn over his earnings to be held in escrow for the victims of his crimes.

As might be expected, Simon & Schuster, joined by an array of ultraliberal media types, began whining and screaming, calling the law unconstitutional, a violation of Hill's right of free speech and the media's freedom of the press.

WLF General Counsel Dan Popeo had a prompt response to their complaints.

Hogwash! The law doesn't stop criminals from telling their stories, nor does it stop the media from printing and broadcasting those stories. It only stops criminals from reaping obscene profits from their crimes while their victims are entitled to damages.

Of course, the "Son of Sam" law didn't even apply to Simon & Schuster's profits, only to Henry Hill's.

But it is thanks in large measure to practices and reactions like Simon & Schuster's that the term "freedom of the press" has come today to mean to many Americans the freedom to distort, to manipulate, to indulge in excess and satisfy incredible greed.

The inescapable fact is that Henry Hill would never have told his story, and given Simon & Schuster the income from a best seller, without the lure of big money.

Popeo added, "That's what's so dangerous about this media greed. It helps fuel criminal excesses.

Don't think for a minute that some sicko holding dozens of people hostage doesn't know that the worse his crime, the more money he stands to get from media fanatics who want to tell his "exclusive" story! So, why kill only one person when you can get more money by killing five? or 10? Or 20?

Does the media care? NO! In fact, while the killings are still happening, it's a good bet that media executives are issuing orders and upping the ante, while media reps stumble over one another in their effort to buy the rights to print or broadcast the story and increase corporate profits.

Corporate profits! Freedom of the press! Do they care if lives are placed in danger? Do they care if national security is threatened? Do they care if reputations are falsely destroyed? Do they care if rapists and murderers earn millions for retelling their criminal stories?

Representing the National Association of Attorneys General, WLF made those same points in the case of *Simon & Schuster v. Members of the New York State Crime Victims Board*.

The court agreed with WLF's position and upheld the constitutionality of the law. An appeals court subsequently reaffirmed that decision.

Undaunted, Simon & Schuster and its media allies petitioned the Supreme Court to hear this case.

The Court agreed and, as this book went to press, WLF (representing seven crime victim organizations and more than 40 members of the New York state legislature) filed its brief in the Supreme Court. A hearing will be held in the fall of 1991 with a decision expected in early 1992.

Criminals Don't Pay?

Perhaps one of the most bizarre cases, at least on the surface, that WLF has been involved in is *Pennsylvania v. Davenport*.

As General Counsel Dan Popeo said at the time, "I thought I'd seen it all, but this one left me stunned."

Edward J. and Debora A. Davenport pled guilty to defrauding the Pennsylvania Department of Public Welfare (DPW) of thousands of dollars. They were sentenced to a year of probation and ordered to make restitution to DPW for the money they had stolen.

But the Davenports never made the first payment. Instead, in the same "clever" style of their original crime, they filed a bankruptcy petition, listing their repayment obligation as an unsecured debt based upon "public assistance overpayment."

The process grew even stranger. When the Probation Department began proceedings against the Davenports for violation of their probation, this charming couple went back to bankruptcy court for protection—and won.

From there, the case went to District Court, where the judge reversed the bankruptcy court's decision and once again ordered the restitution payments to be made.

Really into the swing of things by now, the "bankrupt" Davenports appealed that decision, and the Court of Appeals agreed with them, reversing the District Court decision and basically excusing the criminal restitution order.

When the case was to go before the Supreme Court, WLF was there to assist the Commonwealth of Pennsylvania in the fight for justice.

As Popeo said, at the time, "There's too much at stake not to.

The welfare system in this country already costs Americans far too much money. And it infuriates me that people like the Davenports can rip that system off and get away with it. They should have gone to jail.

In addition to the *Davenport* case itself, WLF was concerned about the precedent it would set.

They argued that, under the terms of the Appeals Court decision, if a criminal were to break into our home and steal our most valuable possessions, even if they got caught and pled guilty, they could simply declare bankruptcy and we would get not one cent in reparation for what was stolen from us.

WLF represented a list of clients that included Congressman Henry J. Hyde, the National Organization for Victim Assistance, the National Victim Center, the Stephanie Roper Committee, the Crime Victims Legal Clinic, Parents of Murdered Children, the Unity Group, and the Maryland Coalition Against Crime.

The Foundation argued that the intent of Congress when it enacted the Bankruptcy Reform Act of 1978 was to prevent convicted criminals from using Chapter 13 of the Bankruptcy Code to avoid paying restitution to their victims. WLF also argued that subsequent Congressional legislation underscored and reinforced that point.

Unfortunately, on May 29, 1990, the Supreme Court dealt a setback to the rights of crime victims to require criminals to pay them restitution, in essence approving the concept that criminals can indeed avoid making such payments by filing for bankruptcy.

Fortunately for those same victims, however, as a result of publicity focused on the *Davenport* case by WLF and others, Congress moved quickly and later that year amended the bankruptcy laws to close the loophole created by the Supreme Court's decision.

Keeping America Free—And Strong

From its very founding, the Washington Legal Foundation, in addition to representing the interests of individual, mainstream honest Americans, has been a steadfast supporter of America's national defense, working to keep our country strong and ready to resist our enemies throughout the world.

In WLF's very first case, when General Counsel Dan Popeo operated out of a one-man office and his wife typed the complaint at home on a typewriter she had from college, they represented 55 Congressmen in a suit against the Carter administration's transfer of control of the Panama Canal to Panama.

Even though they barely lost the suit in a 2–1 appellate ruling, they nonetheless showed from the outset that WLF was a force to be reckoned with in any area of the law, but especially in the areas of national defense and security.

Whether it's the actions of spies or it's Radical Left groups challenging the Government's right to defend us, WLF has been unwavering in its defense of our national security.

Dukakis v. Department of Defense

To many Americans, it would come as no surprise to learn that former Massachusetts Governor and U.S. Presidential candidate Michael S. Dukakis was, during the period of his candidacy, in court challenging the Constitution and trying to emasculate the very office he was hoping to win and endangering America's national security in the process.

But WLF got wind of what Dukakis was up to and, representing 31 U.S. Congressmen, didn't hesitate to jump into the fray opposite Dukakis.

The story behind this strange case has its roots in one simple, also unsurprising fact: Michael Dukakis didn't agree with Ronald Reagan's foreign policy.

The liberation of Grenada, the bombing of Libya (which certainly took the starch out of Khadafi), the bold capture of the *Achille Lauro* terrorists. . . . Governor Dukakis considered each of those actions to be illegal.

But he reserved his special contempt for President Reagan's Central American policies. So, when a unit of the Massachusetts National Guard was ordered to report for a two-week training session in Panama and Honduras, Governor Dukakis objected, saying it would be fine if they went to another area but not to Central America.

Then, in the classic tradition of the Radical Left legal groups, Dukakis went to court to keep "his" national guard at home, claiming that governors, not the President and not Congress, have control over the National Guard.

Fortunately, some judges in this country still respect the constitution, and Federal District Court Judge Robert Keeton ruled against Dukakis, ordering the troops to go.

By the way, the definition of "troops" in this case was 13 members of a public affairs unit. As one member described their function, "Our idea of shooting is taking pictures."

Judge Keeton left little room for doubt about his ruling. In throwing out the case, he described it as one in which "judicial intrusion would hardly be appropriate."

But Governor Dukakis didn't stop there. Despite Judge Keeton's rather unequivocal ruling, Dukakis filed an appeal.

Dukakis' major guru in this case was Laurence Tribe, the Harvard law professor who did such an outstanding job of trashing honor and ethics in his assault on Reagan Supreme Court nominee, Judge Robert Bork.

Dukakis' action showed the same total disregard for the Constitution and the country's national security that Americans have come to expect from the Radical Left.

But, by pursuing the case in the courts, Dukakis took what should have been a political issue and turned it into a legal issue for the courts to decide.

And in the process, he opened the door for WLF to intervene.

Since WLF's number one goal has always been to defend and protect the American people from the efforts of the Radical Left to use our court system to try to destroy this great nation, WLF prepared to go toe-to-toe with Dukakis and his ultraliberal legal cronies all the way to the Supreme Court if necessary.

The battle was made more difficult when left-wing forces with unlimited funds to spend on the effort took Dukakis under their protection and decided to defend him in court. The ACLU, for example, naturally had to look out for one of its most famous "card-carrying members."

Dukakis and his cronies based their challenge to presidential authority on claims that the Montgomery Amendment is unconstitutional. The Montgomery Amendment was passed by Congress in 1986 to deny state governors the power to block overseas training of the National Guard when they object to the location or purpose of the training.

In opposing Dukakis, WLF stressed that the Constitution of the United States vests control of the military and foreign affairs in the federal government, not in state governors, and that the National Guard ceases to be under state control whenever it is called into federal service for training or other purposes.

On October 25, 1988, the U.S. Court of Appeals for the First Circuit sided with WLF's position on this case and upheld Judge Keeton's earlier decision.

Still undaunted, Dukakis continued to pursue his effort, petitioning the Supreme Court to hear the case.

On April 17, 1989, the Supreme Court handed WLF a decisive victory and Dukakis another resounding defeat when it denied the petition for certiorari and declined to review the case.

Dukakis' effort was not the only challenge to the Montgomery Amendment. WLF represented 24 U.S. Senators and Congressmen in another Montgomery Amendment-related case, which did end up before the U.S. Supreme Court.

The case involved a challenge by another "flaky" governor, Rudy Perpich of Minnesota. Perpich, like Dukakis and others, had been an outspoken critic of American foreign policy in Central America and had filed his suit to try and prevent Minnesota

National Guardsmen from being sent on a Defense Department-ordered training exercise in Honduras.

In its Supreme Court brief, WLF argued that the Montgomery Amendment does indeed constitute a valid exercise of Congress' powers under the Army and Militia Clauses of the U.S. Constitution.

Furthermore, WLF attorneys argued that state governors should not be allowed to interfere with U.S. foreign policy, especially when such interference impairs the training necessary to maintain the readiness of military troops.

In June of 1990, the Supreme Court, in a unanimous decision, agreed with WLF's arguments and rejected Perpich's challenge.

Shelter for the "Storm"

As American and Coalition forces were carrying out Operation Desert Storm in the Persian Gulf with an efficiency and dispatch never before witnessed in warfare, Americans looked on not only with tremendous pride but with a renewed respect for America's military capability.

Most Americans, that is. But not all.

Not William Kunstler. Of course this man has had a long-standing hatred for anything that makes people think of America as great. In fact, this man has confessed—no, *boasted*—of being a "double agent, working within the system to destroy the system."

Hardly had the planes begun their precision bombing runs, hardly had the first Tomahawk cruise missiles hit their targets, before Kunstler's Center for Constitutional Rights filed a lawsuit against President George Bush, Defense Secretary Dick Cheney, Chairman of the Joint Chiefs of Staff Colin Powell, and Defense Department Spokesman Pete Williams.

Disturbed by the overwhelming support for the war by the American people, Kunstler and his cronies at the Center for Constitutional Rights wanted to do something to undermine that support. So they filed suit against the Pentagon-ordered restrictions on media coverage of Operation Desert Storm.

Representing a "who's who" of the Radical Left fringe media, they demanded unrestricted access so their clients could report their own unique version of the "news."

These were not even such traditionally liberal publications as *The Washington Post* or *The New York Times*. These were leftist rags like *Mother Jones, The Village Voice, The L.A. Weekly, The Progressive, The Guardian* and others—publications whose only interest in reporting news from the Middle East would have been to attack our efforts there.

They wouldn't care if they endangered the lives of American or Coalition servicemen and women. They wouldn't care if they played right into Saddam Hussein's hands. In fact, most of them would have been glad to help.

That's because publications like those have their own interpretation of journalism and objective reporting.

If they interviewed 100 military personnel and 99 of them were gung-ho, patriotic, "good to go" warriors, and one of them had a few reservations about being over there, they'd report on the one and ignore the other 99.

WLF's concern over the Kunstler group's effort

in this case was increased when it was learned that, in the time-honored tradition of Radical Left legal groups conspiring to get their cases heard by ultraliberal judges, they had managed to have this case heard by none other than the infamous Judge Leonard Sand.

That's the same judge WLF battled against in a Yonkers, N.Y. "housing discrimination" case and who also ruled that panhandling in the New York subways is a form of free speech protected by the first amendment. (See chapter, "Judges Need to Be Reminded of Role in Justice System.")

Kunstler and Sand. A potentially dangerous combination for America.

Of course, as Kunstler should have learned to expect by now, when his case arrived in court, WLF was there too, opposing every move he tried to make.

Even Judge Sand realized that this time Kunstler had gone too far. Although sympathetic with Kunstler's arguments, he dismissed the case.

But the Pentagon's restriction on the media was not the only Desert Storm-related issue that WLF and Kunstler's Center for Constitutional Rights went toe-to-toe on.

Another case centered around a Marine Corporal who, after nearly four years in the Corps, decided he was a conscientious objector. His decision, or "conversion," had by remarkable coincidence occurred when he was ordered to go to Saudi Arabia.

When Corporal Jeffrey Paterson refused to go, the Marines naturally filed charges and initiated court-martial proceedings.

Smelling blood, Kunstler's group sprang immediately into action to defend their new "client." Also, no one seemed surprised when Kunstler's other favorite radical group, the ACLU, jumped into the case with them.

Not only did they try to make sure the Marines couldn't touch their client, they used his case as an excuse to challenge the right of the President of the United States and the right of the Armed Forces, specifically the U.S. Marine Corps, to send our military personnel where they're needed.

It's always an integral part of their plan in cases like this to generate as much coverage by the liberal news media as possible. So, in order to keep Paterson available to the media to tell the touching story of his heartwarming conversion to conscientious objector status, they had to find some means of keeping the Marines from putting him in jail.

Well, just as in the press restriction case, they looked around and found a sympathetic federal judge who, despite a long history of federal courts not interfering with the military justice system, ordered Paterson free (and therefore accessible to the media for countless repetitive interviews) until his court martial.

When the Marine Corps appealed that decision, Kunstler's group and the ACLU teamed up again and found an appeals court judge who would side with them once again.

And, in an even more important step, these radicals worked to prevent a court-martial of Paterson entirely, by claiming that the Marines' order to send Paterson to Saudi Arabia was illegal and that he could not therefore be convicted.

Representing a roster of U.S. Congressmen,

WLF entered into this and a similar case, *Ange v. Bush*, arguing for the President's right to send troops to the Middle East without first obtaining a declaration of war from Congress.

While the likes of William Kunstler were arguing that the orders exceeded the President's authority under the War Powers Clause of the Constitution and the War Powers Resolution, WLF was arguing that the political question doctrine precluded the courts from addressing those issues and that the President had not exceeded his authority.

Fortunately, this time the courts accepted WLF's argument and threw the challenges out of court.

There were numerous other challenges from the Radical Left to Operation Desert Storm. Ralph Nader's Public Citizen filed suit to prevent our military leaders from using measures that would protect military personnel from the chemical and biological warfare people had reason to believe Saddam Hussein would not hesitate to use.

Ramsey Clark showed up on television from Baghdad moaning and howling about the "atrocities" America was committing in the region. (He was so bad that even CNN cut him off.)

The ACLU and others encouraged our military personnel to desert. They tried to recruit spies from within the military and from within numerous government agencies—anyone at all who could perhaps deliver any information that could be used to discredit America's efforts in the Middle East.

On every front and in every arena, WLF met those challenges.

Dangers from Within

Operation Desert Storm proved to the entire world that the United States is capable of mobilizing its military might anywhere in the world to resist enemy attacks.

But what about America's ability to defend itself from enemies here at home? How does America deal with spies in her midst who give away or sell secrets to the highest bidder?

WLF has left little doubt over the years as to where it stands on spies.

In the infamous Walker spy trial, for example, WLF gained great visibility with its courtroom arguments that the death penalty was the only appropriate sentence for the ringleader of that sorry episode, John Walker, and his accomplices, for selling secrets to the Soviets.

WLF believed then and believes today that the death penalty should be imposed for espionage and treason.

The Walkers—John Anthony Walker, Jr., a retired Navy chief communications officer, his son Michael, brother Arthur, and a friend named Jerry Whitworth—were accused of passing classified information to the Soviet Union.

Government officials admitted that the spy ring had done serious damage to the Navy's communication system and our national security, but they declined to press for the death penalty. Thus, it fell to WLF to enter the case to argue that the defendants should receive the death penalty for their crimes, as provided by federal law.

It was noted that the last people executed under

death penalty provisions contained in the Espionage Act were Ethel and Julius Rosenberg in 1953.

WLF continues to push for capital punishment for spies like the Walkers.

Spying for the Media

Of course, if a spy can't find a foreign government willing to pay for information and secrets, there's always the news media.

Samuel Loring Morison found out what a lucrative practice that could be, selling military secrets to the news media.

Morison was an employee of the Naval Intelligence Command. His specialty was in Soviet ship analysis.

In the summer of 1984, Morison illegally took classified documents from his Navy office, including several spy satellite photographs clearly marked "secret."

He cut off the "secret" designation and turned the photographs over to his contacts with a foreign publication.

After they were printed in Morison's selected foreign publication, they were later picked up by *The Washington Post*, CBS-TV, and others.

Morison was subsequently arrested and prosecuted under the espionage statutes for divulging national security secrets. In December, 1985, he was convicted and sentenced to two years in prison.

Naturally, he appealed. And it was in his appeal that this case took on an even greater significance. He was aided not only by the ACLU, which would be expected, but by a coalition of news media organizations that left Dan Popeo and WLF feeling, in his words, "like David taking on Goliath."

To explain that statement, here's the full list of those news organizations that supported Morison's appeal:

The Washington Post, CBS, Inc., National Broadcasting Company, Inc., Capital Cities/ABC, Inc., Time Inc., Newsweek, U.S. News & World Report, The Wall Street Journal, The New York Times, The New York Daily News, The Los Angeles Times, The Chicago Tribune, The Boston Globe, The Atlanta Journal and Constitution, The Miami Herald, The Dallas Morning News, The Minneapolis Star and Tribune, Ottoway Newspapers, Inc., The Associated Press, National Public Radio, Pulitzer Broadcasting Company, The American Society of Newspaper Editors, The American Newspaper Publishers Association, The American Booksellers Association, Inc., Associated Press Managing Editors, The Magazine Publishers Association, The National Association of Broadcasters, The Newspaper Guild, The Radio-Television News Directors Association, The Reporters Committee for Freedom of the Press, and The Society of Professional Journalists.

The news media obviously were determined to secure for themselves the right to receive and publish such classified information (since it would help sell papers and boost broadcast ratings) whenever and wherever the opportunity presented itself.

But all of Morison's supporters and his claims to First Amendment protection for his actions were not enough: The United States Court of Appeals for the Fourth Circuit handed WLF a major victory by rejecting those First Amendment arguments and unanimously upholding Samuel Loring Morison's convictions for espionage and theft of government property. The Supreme Court later rejected Morison's appeal.

"NO" to the PLO

Well, since they weren't allowed free and unfettered use of spies to help bring down America, maybe the best thing to do is to invite terrorists in to operate freely on our own soil.

That certainly seemed to be the case in 1987 when the PLO, at the time the world's deadliest terrorist group, had an "office" in Washington, D.C.

Yes, Yassir Arafat's beloved Palestine Liberation Organization, a band of cutthroat murderers if ever there was one, had an "information office" literally within shooting distance of the White House.

Some of WLF's clients, including Senator Jesse Helms and then U.S. Representative Jack Kemp, pressured the State Department into ordering the office to be closed.

That seemed like a wise move at the time, considering all circumstances.

But it was met with outrage by the ACLU. In their accustomed knee-jerk fashion, they started yammering about First Amendment guarantees and went to court to prevent the closing.

Predictably, their actions ignited a firestorm of controversy. After all, the PLO had been on a worldwide rampage of terror and violence for two decades—and had openly declared the U.S.A. to be their enemy and therefore a target for their terrorist acts.

The "office" in question was called the Palestine Information Office, operated by a naturalized American citizen named Hassan Abdul Rahman. It functioned exclusively on behalf of the PLO which provided several hundred thousand dollars a year to fund it.

Part of that money went for Rahman to visit America's classrooms to spread the PLO's propaganda message.

Similar "information offices" in other world capitals had been "safe houses" from which terrorist attacks were launched, or arms caches with huge stockpiles of weapons.

One Palestinian expert in Scotland said, "There are several kinds of people employed in PLO offices," and "They are all ready to do violence."

Of course, the PLO is the organization which had already claimed the credit for—and bragged about—the murder of at least 32 Americans and the injury of even more.

The same organization that, when Mohammed Abu Abbas ordered Leon Klinghofer shot in his wheelchair and thrown overboard during the hijacking of the *Achille Lauro,* rewarded his actions by naming him to the PLO executive committee.

And of course, the same organization that placed its support and hopes so firmly in Saddam Hussein's camp during Operation Desert Storm.

When the executive director of the ACLU announced his group was supporting this band of thugs, he said, "I'm afraid even the good guys on civil liberties are going to be against us on this one."

Well, WLF was certainly against them and, representing a list of clients that included three U.S. Senators and 13 U.S. Representatives, WLF set out once again to battle the ACLU.

WLF had another client in this case, however, the family of Robert Stethem.

Robbie Stethem was the young Navy diver who was in the wrong place at the wrong time during the hijacking of TWA Flight 847 in 1985.

He was brutally beaten, tortured, and thrown from the airplane to bleed to death on the Beirut tarmac.

After Robbie's cruel and senseless death, the Stethems were reassured by many, including President and Mrs. Reagan, that Robbie's death would not be in vain, that his killers would be brought to justice, and that the U.S. would take strong action against terrorists everywhere.

The Stethems certainly didn't consider allowing the PLO to operate freely within our nation's capital to be "taking strong action against terrorists."

In a statement they issued at the time, they noted:

Robbie suffered an extremely painful death. Alone and bleeding, he was left to die on the airport runway in a foreign country. Young marines have been burned alive far away from home and families. An elderly gentleman was shot and thrown overboard, helpless to survive. Are we to allow PLO representatives to get a foothold on our soil? Are we to allow them to continue working, living and enjoying American freedoms and our

way of life and at the same time, finance terror and PLO policies?
We say "No!"

WLF said "No!" too. And U.S. District Court Judge Charles R. Richey listened. And agreed.

Judge Richey turned down the ACLU and let the State Department-ordered closing stand.

Practically before the courtroom had a chance to clear, the ACLU announced its intention to file an appeal on an expedited basis.

On August 5, 1988, the U.S. Court of Appeals for the D.C. Circuit once again agreed with WLF that the U.S. government has the right to close down the PLO's "information" office.

Ramsey and Moammar

Of course, it was not only the ACLU that came down on the side of anti-American terrorists—they had company.

In 1986, Americans and freedom-loving people throughout the world were celebrating the April air strike ordered by President Reagan against the headquarters of that Libyan mad dog, Moammar Khadafy, in response to a series of Khadafy-ordered terrorist actions.

And celebrate they should, since that strike has proved to this very day to be one of the most effective counterattacks against terrorism the world has ever seen.

Not everyone was celebrating, however. Not even every American.

Ramsey Clark wasn't. This man, who was once

the highest ranking law enforcement officer in the United States, who as Attorney General in the Johnson Administration took an oath to uphold the law and protect the American people, proved to be more interested in helping those who want to destroy the American people.

He raced to Libya as soon as possible after the air strike and met with Khadafy himself to discuss options. Out of that meeting came the decision to file a lawsuit on behalf of a selected group of Khadafy's Libyans against the United States of America, and specifically President Reagan.

U.S. District Court Judge Thomas Penfield Jackson dismissed Clark's lawsuit against his own country and described it as an attempt to use the court for a public protest.

Clark decided to appeal Judge Jackson's decision. When he did, WLF was there to oppose him, representing five members of Congress and the Allied Educational Foundation.

WLF urged the appeals court to see this lawsuit for what it was and to uphold Judge Jackson's original decision.

A three-judge federal appeals court in the District of Columbia agreed, saying, "We do not conceive it a proper function of a federal court to serve as a forum for protests, to the detriment of parties with serious disputes waiting to be heard."

The appeals court then ordered Judge Jackson to impose monetary sanctions on Clark for bringing a frivolous lawsuit against the United States—the application of an increasingly powerful weapon against the Radical Left's abuse of the court system.

(See the chapter, "Battling Back: A New Weapon in the War.")

Lawyer for the Little Guy

That headline appeared on a feature article written about Dan Popeo and the Washington Legal Foundation several years ago.

It summed up then and continues to sum up today a very important component of WLF's overall activities.

As America's Voice in the Courts, WLF has often been there for mainstream Americans when no one else could or would be there.

For small business owners, for individuals or groups who had been seriously wronged by the courts or by an out-of-control bureaucracy, for municipalities faced with irresponsible litigation by Radical Left legal groups seeking to advance their own cause, WLF has frequently been the only resource, the last hope.

Out of dozens of similar cases WLF has pursued over the years, however, perhaps none bear more eloquent testimony to this particular role than the stories which follow. They tell of three loyal Americans—two immigrants who fled to this country to escape communist tyranny in their homeland and the other who fought for America's freedom during World War II.

Ensnared by the long arms of the KGB

There were a lot of protests going on in Washington, D.C., during January, 1985.

In front of the South African embassy, for example, hundreds of people gathered on a daily basis to protest that nation's "evil" policies.

Among the luminaries participating in those protests were the likes of Amy Carter, Teddy Kennedy, Jesse Jackson, Lowell Weicker, and other darlings of the liberal media.

They were loud. Marching. Chanting. Shouting. Waving banners. Generally creating the kind of media circus they have become expert at and so well known for.

Meanwhile, a few blocks away, a woman small in stature but large in heart was standing in lonely solitary vigil on the sidewalk outside the Russian embassy.

Her name was Vanna Om Strinko.

Vanna was born in Cambodia. She worked for the United States embassy there until the communists took over in 1975.

Over 3 million of her fellow Cambodians were slaughtered in the reign of terror that followed, including most of Vanna's own family.

Vanna was evacuated with other U.S. embassy personnel and came to the United States. Here she wasted no time in forming an organization that would help resettle other Cambodian and Vietnamese refugees who were fleeing the tyranny and terror of the communists.

As she stood her lonely vigil in January, 1985, Vanna was an American citizen and a loyal patriot. But she was still distraught with the way the communists had invaded and controlled her native homeland.

Vanna admits that she was afraid as she conducted her one-woman silent protest outside the Russian embassy. She later recalled the thoughts that went through her head that day.

"I remember being frightened, as I thought about how the Russians had provided military support for the communists there (Cambodia), to think that the Soviet Union had the power to reach into a far away land like Cambodia and make such evil things happen."

But, if Vanna Om Strinko had trouble believing the Russians were powerful enough to affect events in her homeland of Cambodia, imagine what she must have thought about the things that happened to her next.

Imagine the new feelings of terror this woman must have felt when she was handcuffed, thrown into a paddy wagon, and hauled off through the streets of Washington, D.C.—the capital of the free world.

Worse, she was booked, prosecuted, convicted, and sentenced to jail.

Meanwhile, the Kennedys, Carters, Jacksons, and others continued to carry on their raucous protests outside the South African embassy with total and complete immunity from any prosecution.

It was one of the worst cases of selective prosecution ever witnessed in this country, so blatant that even the ultraliberal *Washington Post* was troubled by Vanna's arrest and prosecution, commenting twice on the matter in editorials.

Part of one editorial offered this:

"Talk about inconsistent treatment of demonstrators in the capital of the free world: Some 1,655 people are charged with breaking a law by demonstrating within 500 feet of the South African Embassy and [the U.S. Attorney] has all federal charges dropped before anybody even goes to court. Three other people do the same thing in front of the British Embassy and they, too, go free with charges dropped. Then one woman is arrested for the same offense in front of the Soviet Embassy—and [the U.S. Attorney] proceeds to prosecute her. Can you explain the difference?"

Unfortunately, the difference was made clear when it was learned that D.C. officials did not want to prosecute protestors at the South African embassy because they believed South Africa was evil and deserved to be the target of such demonstrations.

Furthermore, the federal prosecutor pursuing Mrs. Strinko with such aggression admitted that, with the urging of the State Department, he considered the wishes of Russian embassy personnel—which translates into the initials KGB.

Imagine the public outrage that would arise if U.S. government officials were found to be taking orders from the KGB. It's pretty close to that state of affairs when a federal prosecutor bases his prosecutorial decisions on KGB desires.

And Vanna Om Strinko was the target of those KGB orders.

She was helpless. She couldn't afford to hire one of D.C.'s prestigious law firms to fight for her defense.

And while the ACLU and other leftist legal groups would have eagerly championed the cause of any one of those protestors at the South African embassy, they certainly didn't make a move to help Vanna get the justice she deserved, that she had a right to as an American citizen.

As she described it, "What was most frightening, however, was that no one in the great United States of America seemed to care what the Russians were doing to me—until I met the wonderful people at the Washington Legal Foundation."

She added that "without their constant help and support, I have no doubt at all that I'd be in jail right now."

Vanna Om Strinko had become the first person in over a decade to be prosecuted under a federal law for merely congregating in front of the Soviet embassy.

WLF's litigation strategy was to defend Vanna by arguing both that the statute was unconstitutional and that Mrs. Strinko was being selectively prosecuted.

Soon after Vanna's prosecution, other anti-Soviet protestors, representatives of Jewish groups and other ethnic organizations, also began to be prosecuted and convicted for the same "crime."

As a result of WLF's courtroom involvement in Vanna's case, congressional hearings were subsequently held on this issue, during the summer of 1986.

At those hearings, WLF attorneys testified opposite the U.S. Attorney and a State Department Legal Advisor. Under close examination, the two federal officials admitted that the wishes of the embassy played a critical role in their decisions about whom to prosecute.

However, evidence uncovered by Senator Grassley, who held the hearings, revealed that the South African embassy did nothing to interfere with prosecutorial decisions made about the anti-South African protestors, and suggested strongly that the Russians actively pressured the State Department and the Department of Justice to clamp down on Mrs. Strinko and other anti-Soviet protestors.

It took over three years before Mrs. Strinko's case was finally resolved.

Victory came in the form of a court order in *Strinko v. United States*, which was signed by Associate Judge Shellie F. Bowers on May 13, 1988, ordering that the prosecution be dropped.

That court order came as a result of Supreme Court action in a related civil action challenging the anti-protest law, *Boos v. Barry*. WLF also participated in that case; on March 22, 1988, the Supreme Court held that the law was indeed unconstitutional when applied to peaceful protests as opposed to demonstrations that block the entrances of the embassy or interfere with embassy personnel.

Vanna Om Strinko finally saw justice. And she saw that the Russians couldn't control her here as the communists controlled her homeland. She was extremely grateful for the help she received from the Washington Legal Foundation, who "stood with me from the beginning and stayed with me every step of the way."

"To them, and to those wonderful American people who support them and make it possible for them to help people like me, I will always be grateful."

"Thanks to them, I understand what it means to be an American."

The American Dream Turns into a Nightmare

John Pozsgai also managed to escape the communists who took over his country. In his case, he was forced to flee his native Hungary more than 30 years ago.

What happened to John Pozsgai was described in one account as follows:

"When they came to take him away, John Pozsgai didn't know what was happening to him.

"Without warning, a swarm of police and law enforcement officers arrived at his home, shouting statements he couldn't fully understand, slapped handcuffs on him, threw him into the back of a police car and hauled him away."

Probably not such an uncommon event in Hungary during the 1950s. But the events described did not take place in Hungary. Nor did they take place in the 1950s. They took place in America. In 1988.

There's no doubt that visions of the streets of the Hungary he had fled flashed through his mind, the fear that gripped him during the brutal 1956 communist takeover once again took control of him.

Nor is there any doubt that those feelings didn't fade at all as the events continued to unfold.

John Pozsgai was forced through a trial that was a mockery of justice, but which, in the finest police state tradition, involved secret surveillance and hidden videocameras.

As a result of the "evidence" obtained through those means, he was convicted, sentenced to three years in prison, and fined more than $200,000!

What was this man's crime?

John Pozsgai believed in the American dream and believed he had a chance to live that dream. That was his crime.

He scraped together every penny he could save over the years to buy a piece of land, land that had been used as a dumpsite for over 20 years, land that was not only an eyesore but a health hazard, filled with, among other junk and debris, thousands of filthy used automobile and truck tires.

And he cleaned up that piece of land.

It was for that "crime" that John Pozsgai was hauled away—in handcuffs—by the police.

John had seen something in that dumpsite, that 14-acre piece of garbage-filled land that others didn't see. He saw his future, he saw security for his family.

This was what he had dreamed of during 30 years of hard work, 30 years of scrimping and saving every penny he could; that parcel of land was John Pozsgai's chance at his piece of the American dream, the place where he could expand his own business.

John is a mechanic, a truck mechanic, and by all accounts a good one. And like so many others who fled tyranny and oppression to come to America, he worked hard, put in long, hard hours 7 days a week without complaint in a small garage behind his house, grateful only for the chance to earn a decent living and support his wife and children.

And, after 30 years, he had put aside enough money for a modest downpayment. So he mortgaged his house and property, to raise the rest of the money he needed, and bought that dumpsite.

John Pozsgai planned to open his own garage.

Every spare hour he had was spent working on his land, cleaning it up. He hauled away the 7,000 tires that had been dumped on it over the years, and gradually removed the rest of the debris.

Then he started bringing in clean fill and topsoil to level the part of the property where he planned to build his garage to expand his tiny business.

He loved taking his only grandchild, named after him ("Little John"), to watch the progress, to show him with pride the place where he would build his garage.

But it was not to be.

Because, just as John Pozsgai saw something in that garbage-filled dumpsite that others didn't see, governmental bureaucrats saw something else, too.

Those thousands of filthy used tires had been tossed recklessly into a small stream that had then backed up and flooded John's property.

To everyone in the area, it was nothing more than a breeding ground for mosquitoes, in addition to being an eyesore.

But to some incredible minds at the Army Corps of Engineers and the Environmental Protection Agency, the area flooded by those tires was now technically a *wetland*.

And John Pozsgai had, to their incomparable way of thinking, committed the heinous crime of destroying a wetland. So they charged him with 41 counts of filling in a wetland without a permit.

This was no bay, no marsh, no creek, just a dirty little backup of water created by 7,000 filthy automobile and truck tires in a developed area of town, zoned for light industrial uses near Trenton, New Jersey.

The prosecutor, however, armed with videotapes gathered by the EPA's secret surveillance, bragged that he was going to use John as an example.

His "logic" was that by seeking an extremely punitive sentence for this hard-working Hungarian immigrant who had very little money and a wife with heart trouble who still struggles with the complexity of the English language, he'd be sending a message, as he put it, to "all private property owners," land developers, and the business world that corporate officers will be sent to jail for "environmental" violations.

This overzealous prosecutor then found a sympathetic ally in Judge Marvin Katz, described by one source as a "wild-eyed liberal," who also wanted to make an example of John Pozsgai.

And their combined determination to destroy this man resulted in a sentence of three years in prison and a fine of $202,000.

This was the largest sentence and largest fine ever imposed on an individual in the history of the United States for *any* environmental violation, and yet not a single fish, bird, or sea lion was killed or harmed; indeed, the tiny stream runs clearer thanks to John's clean-up efforts.

As soon as the Washington Legal Foundation learned of John Pozsgai's plight, they immediately filed for an appeal of his conviction and sentence to the Third U.S. Circuit Court of Appeals.

Incredibly, that court upheld the conviction without holding oral arguments and without stating any reasons for its decision!

WLF and John Pozsgai then filed a petition for writ of certiorari with the U.S. Supreme Court, asking them to review the lower courts' actions.

While they were waiting for the Supreme Court's decision, the U.S. Department of Justice filed a brief with the court candidly admitting that it had misrepresented crucial evidence in the Court of Appeals in order to sustain John Pozsgai's conviction.

The Justice Department brief admitted, among

other things, that the Assistant U.S. Attorney in Philadelphia "advised the jury in his opening statement that he would be offering direct evidence to establish [key jurisdictional facts], but apparently because of an oversight that evidence was never introduced."

On appeal, the Justice Department had argued that the jurisdictional facts—that Pozsgai's property was adjacent to a stream that was a tributary of the Pennsylvania Canal and that the canal was used in interstate commerce—could be gleaned from two aerial photographs which allegedly showed the jury that the "stream flows into the canal."

These photographs had been inexplicably missing from the district court file room when Paul D. Kamenar, WLF's Executive Legal Director, attempted to examine them to verify the Justice Department's assertion.

When they were eventually returned long after the briefing was completed, it was discovered that the photos do not show any stream at all on the property, let alone one flowing into the canal.

Attempts by WLF to get the Justice Department to correct the record in the court of appeals were rebuffed, and that court subsequently affirmed the sentence.

It was only after WLF attorneys met with representatives of the Solicitor General's office, supported by photographs WLF had had taken at considerable expense, that the Solicitor General finally admitted in his brief filed with the Supreme Court, "The government's brief in the court of appeals asserted that the aerial photographs introduced at trial showed the stream flowing into the canal. That representation, we have now determined, was inaccurate. We have examined the photographs and determined that they do not show the stream flowing into the canal."

The brief concluded on that point by saying, "In sum, the record is admittedly quite thin with regard to the two elements needed to establish federal jurisdiction" over Pozsgai's property.

Unfortunately, even this admission of misrepresented evidence wasn't enough. The Supreme Court decided not to review the case.

As this book was prepared for press, John Pozsgai was an inmate at Allenwood Federal Prison.

But WLF has still refused to abandon this man and continues to explore every possible angle to secure his release.

According to government documents, John would have gotten a lighter sentence if he was manager of a crack house, had stolen a car, or had committed larceny or any number of serious offenses.

In addition to filing post-conviction motions, WLF is also actively gathering signatures on a petition to be sent to President Bush calling for a commutation of sentence.

Plus, WLF is representing John in parallel civil proceedings, and is seeking an after-the-fact permit from Pennsylvania's environmental agencies.

Whatever it takes, WLF is determined to help restore John Pozsgai's piece of the American dream.

Burn it but don't fly it?

Two events in America in 1989 focused on the American flag. The Washington Legal Foundation was deeply involved in both.

America's Voice in the Courts

One, and the one which by far drew the greatest attention, was the stunning decision by the U.S. Supreme Court, in *Texas v. Johnson*, that said that avowed communist Gregory Lee "Joey" Johnson did indeed have a First Amendment right to burn the American flag.

Naturally, groups like the American Civil Liberties Union had been involved in Johnson's defense for years.

Yet, even before the Supreme Court's decision, as the Justices were deliberating in that case, the ACLU and other groups were asked for help by another American who was involved in a flag case.

An American World War II Navy veteran named Lee Bach.

Bach, it seems, had gotten himself in trouble for the unbelievable crime of—flying the American flag in front of his home. A neighbor claimed that the flapping of Old Glory in the breeze violated a town anti-noise ordinance!

Imagine, in the wave of patriotism that followed Operation Desert Storm, someone coming into conflict with the law for flying the flag.

But the ACLU refused to help him. And a New Mexico judge found him guilty!

It was then that this courageous Navy vet, who was facing a jail term of 90 days and a fine for flag-flying, asked the Washington Legal Foundation for help.

It's in many ways a story that is so typical of the dilemma that faces America today, that helps to tear America apart.

What made this case so engrossing, so much a test of the American system, was the stark contrast between the two individuals involved.

Joey Johnson is a member of the Revolutionary Communist Youth Brigade and considers America to be "a sick and dying empire," for which he has no respect at all, even after the Supreme Court decision finding he was not at fault.

The day he burned the American flag in Dallas, Johnson had led his scruffy band of hoodlums on a rampage of destruction and violence. They capped their little spree by shouting anti-American obscenities as they set fire to a flag that his thugs had stolen from a flagpole along their way.

Lee Bach, on the other hand, is proud of his country and proud of his service in her defense.

Yet Joey Johnson had Radical Left legal groups lining up to defend him for burning the American flag, and Lee Bach couldn't find anyone to stand up for him, to defend his Constitutional rights—except for the Washington Legal Foundation.

That's what made Lee Bach's case so galling for Dan Popeo and others at WLF. Because the very next day after Bach was convicted for flying the flag, Joey Johnson was shown on nationwide television celebrating his victory by setting fire to another American flag.

Equally galling to the WLF attorneys and to decent Americans everywhere was the appearance of William Kunstler, who took over Johnson's case before the Supreme Court, yammering on and on about this "great victory for civil rights."

The Kunstlers of this country can always be found protecting the "civil rights" of anti-American radicals like Joey Johnson.

WLF can be found protecting the real civil rights

of decent, honest, mainstream Americans like Lee Bach.

Fortunately, this time WLF was able to convince the court to schedule an expedited appeal and, working around the clock, the attorneys on the case mounted a legal defense for Lee Bach.

Even more fortunately, there are still some judges who haven't bought into the Radical Left's agenda; as a packed courtroom cheered, Bach's conviction was overturned.

Protecting the Civil Rights of *All* Americans

It sometimes surprises people to hear Washington Legal Foundation described as one of America's leading groups in the fight for civil rights.

That's because the liberals in the news media, acting hand in glove with Radical Left legal groups and ultraliberal judges, have done an incredible job of molding the public perception that civil rights and discrimination cases only focus on the "wrongs," real or perceived, done to blacks and members of other minority groups by whites.

That perception is wrong. Totally wrong.

The Civil Rights Act of 1964 was intended to give every American the chance at a job, at a promotion, at an education—regardless of the color of his or her skin.

Unfortunately, what was intended is not what is happening, and in 1991, individuals throughout America continue to suffer the sting of discrimination because of their skin color.

Reverse discrimination has joined discrimination against minorities and women as a problem in our society.

As America, guided by groups like the ACLU and the NAACP Legal Defense Fund and others, has set out to correct the abuses of the past, they have gone entirely too far in the other direction and created a whole new set of abuses.

Hiring practices, promotion requirements, college admission standards, scholarship award criteria, which if they were as biased in favor of white males would be blatantly illegal and forced immediately to be discontinued, are regularly used to guarantee women and other minority group members favorable treatment.

Washington Legal Foundation has long been a leader in fighting such blatant examples of reverse discrimination.

Reverse Discrimination in Richmond

People are often amazed at the cases that even make it to court at all—and even more at those that end up before the U.S. Supreme Court.

These are cases that seem so cut and dried that it's difficult to find any reason whatsoever for the case to be tried before the Supreme Court.

In WLF's eyes, *City of Richmond v. J.A. Croson Company* was one of those cases.

In 1983, the City of Richmond, Virginia, Capital of the Confederacy, enacted a reverse-discrimination statute that basically required 30 percent of all city contracts to be awarded to minority businesses.

The "logic" behind the statute was that, with a 50 percent black population, it was reasonable to insist that 30 percent of all city contracts be awarded to minority businesses.

(The Fourth Circuit Court of Appeals, in a stinging ruling that the statute was a blatant violation of the Equal Protection Clause of the Fourteenth Amendment, described that 30 percent figure as having "emerged from the mists.")

A year after this remarkable statute was enacted, the city asked for bids on a plumbing contract at the city jail. The J.A. Croson company was the only bidder.

Yet the city rejected Croson's bid for the project because the company was not owned by Eskimos, Blacks, Aleuts, or Indians.

In other words, Croson was denied the right to be the successful bidder, despite the fact that there was not one other bidder, because its owners were the wrong color.

An examination of the Richmond statute showed that even if there were good intentions behind the program, it was difficult to see how it could ever have benefitted Richmond's citizens, minority or otherwise.

That's because there proved to be a lack of qualified minority firms in the area. So, in order to satisfy the 30 percent requirement, firms had to use subcontractors from Atlanta or Philadelphia.

Even Croson, in the case in question, tried to save the project by seeking bids from subcontractors as far away as North Dakota.

All that means is that money which could have been kept in Richmond to benefit the city's economy was instead being spent in other cities and states.

That's how programs like Richmond's and others like it all over the country actually hurt the very people they are intended to help, both by spending construction dollars outside the city and by unnecessarily inflating construction costs.

What makes such construction programs so absurd in the first place is that they set out to correct abuse that never existed.

The competitive bidding process is inherently non-discriminatory: sealed bids are opened and the contract is awarded strictly on the basis of the lowest bid.

Furthermore, in Richmond's case, the black city council members who designed the plan made no specific findings of past discrimination to justify their actions.

All of those facts and more were cited by the U.S. Court of Appeals for the Fourth Circuit.

Yet, even after its resounding defeat there, Richmond still persisted in taking its case to the Supreme Court.

The reason why was simple. At that time, there were 36 states and 190 local jurisdictions with similar set-aside programs on their books.

And they didn't want those pet programs thrown out, even if they were discriminatory and even if they were costing taxpayers hundreds of thousands of dollars in higher contracting costs.

So they lined up behind Richmond, to offer their support—and their financial clout. Naturally the ACLU jumped in. So did the NAACP and NOW and other familiar faces of the Radical Left, groups whose influence had led to the adoption of reverse discrimination programs like this in the first place.

But there were other players in this one, too. A total of 53 different organizations, to be exact, including such groups as the Mexican-American Legal Defense and Educational Fund, the Louisiana Association of Minority and Women Owned Businesses, Inc., the San Francisco Black Chamber of Commerce, and Alpha Kappa Alpha Sorority, among others.

WLF, in addition to supporting Croson before the Supreme Court, was representing the Lincoln

Institute for Research and Education, a group which, among other works, publishes the *Lincoln Review,* a journal with articles by black scholars who oppose government solutions to minority problems and instead offer free-market and self-help approaches to improve the economic status of minorities.

In its Supreme Court brief, WLF essentially asked the justices to reject Richmond's case as nothing more than fuzzy thinking and statistical voodoo to justify a politically motivated racial spoils system that was morally wrong, that violated fundamental notions of fairness and denied equal protection of the law.

In a 6–3 vote which received considerable attention nationwide, the Supreme Court did just that and struck down Richmond's set-aside program. The decision also sent a warning to all those other 225 programs that cities and localities must prove a history of specific bias against black bidders to justify such drastic steps.

Patterson v. McLean Credit Union

If WLF felt outnumbered in the City of Richmond reverse discrimination case when there were 53 groups and individuals on the opposite side, that was nothing compared to their involvement in *Patterson v. McLean Credit Union,* when over 60 U.S. Senators, more than 100 U.S. Representatives, and over 100 "civil rights" groups joined hands—and checkbooks—on the opposite side from WLF.

What had the ultraliberals so upset was the Supreme Court's 1988 announcement that it planned to use the *Patterson* case to reconsider its ruling in a

1976 case, *Runyon v. McCrary*. *Runyon* is a decision near and dear to the hearts of the Left, and they came out in droves to defend it.

In addition to the usual cast of characters, there were groups practically no one had heard from before. They ran the leftist gamut from the ACLU to the National Gay and Lesbian Task Force, from the NAACP to the American-Arab Anti-Discrimination Committee.

And the individual overseeing all this resistance, the one person pulling all these ultraliberal forces together was none other than the senator from the People's Republic of Massachusetts, that paragon of morality and leadership by example, Teddy Kennedy.

Kennedy's plan was simple—to use the same political clout that torpedoed Judge Bork's Supreme Court nomination to intimidate the Supreme Court into seeing things his way.

What got lost in all the Left's handwringing over the issue was that the Supreme Court's 1976 *Runyon* decision is one of the most ill-considered civil rights cases on the books.

Runyon held that the Civil Rights Act of 1866 (no, that's not a typo, 1866 is correct) prohibits racial discrimination by any person making any contract, whether it be employment or otherwise. What made the decision extraordinary was that in the previous 110 years that the law (known popularly as Section 1981) had been on the books, no court had ever interpreted the law that way.

Everyone previously had interpreted the law as merely giving blacks equal access to courts to enforce their contracts. No court had ever held that Section 1981 applied to discrimination by individuals.

Indeed, it was because Section 1981 was thought not to apply to private discrimination that civil rights leaders fought so hard for passage of the Civil Rights Act of 1964. But, while the 1964 law outlawed racial discrimination in employment, the law contained numerous safeguards to ensure that employers did not become overburdened with frivolous and harassing lawsuits by disgruntled employees.

For example, the 1964 law requires employees to have their discrimination claims mediated by the Equal Employment Opportunity Commission before they can file a lawsuit. Any claim must be brought within six months, or it is barred—thereby eliminating stale claims. An employee who prevails in his discrimination claim can obtain reinstatement and back wages, but he may not recover "pain and suffering" damages and punitive damages.

All those reasonable safeguards were eliminated by the *Runyon* decision. By interpreting Section 1981 as outlawing private racial discrimination, the Court permitted employees to make an end-run around those safeguards by filing their employment discrimination lawsuits under Section 1981 rather than under the Civil Rights Act of 1964.

All of a sudden, employers were faced with multi-million dollar lawsuits; even if they had done nothing wrong, they had to settle, and agree to give preferences to minority employees, rather than risk the possibility of losing a lawsuit that could bankrupt their company.

That's why the Court, when given another opportunity to interpret Section 1981, seized the chance to reconsider its *Runyon* decision. And that's why the quota lobby and plaintiffs' attorneys—who had used *Runyon* to turn Section 1981 into a money printing machine—were so up in arms.

Undaunted by the forces arrayed against it, WLF lined up a powerful coalition of its own that supported overruling *Runyon*. WLF in this case represented U.S. Senators Gordon Humphrey, Steve Symms, and Jesse Helms; U.S. Congressmen Jack Kemp (today Secretary of Housing and Urban Development), Henry Hyde, Norman Shumway, Robert Walker, George Wortley, and Robert Dannemeyer; and the Allied Educational Foundation and the Lincoln Institute for Research and Education.

The Supreme Court's June 15, 1989 5–4 decision in *Patterson*, while declining to overrule *Runyon* outright, cut back significantly on the scope of *Runyon*. The Court held that while Section 1981 still applied to discrimination in the "formation" of contracts (such as discrimination in the hiring process), it did not apply to on-the-job discrimination or discriminatory discharges.

Indeed, the Court all but admitted that *Runyon* had been a mistake. It made clear that it was declining to overrule *Runyon* outright not because *Runyon* was correctly decided, but because the decision had been around long enough that it should be up to Congress to change the law if Congress believed that the court had misinterpreted Section 1981.

Patterson was a significant victory for WLF, because it undid much of the damage inflicted by *Runyon*. In most cases, employees who claim they are the victims of racial discrimination must once again file their claims under the Civil Rights Act of

1964, rather than avoiding that law's established procedures by filing a lawsuit under Section 1981.

"A field goal instead of a touchdown" is how WLF's Alan Slobodin described the *Patterson* decision to the national news media the day the decision was announced. *Patterson* was not the total victory WLF had hoped for, because the Court didn't abandon *Runyon* completely. But given the forces lined up against WLF in *Patterson*, WLF has much to be proud of in the outcome of that case.

Discrimination in Scholarships

In colleges and universities all across America, and in the the workplace as well, white Americans today are victims of racial discrimination in its most basic—and illegal—form.

If a college were to announce a new scholarship "for whites only—black students need not apply," there would be a firestorm of controversy and protest.

Every liberal, every "civil rights" group, and and every Radical Left legal group would scream bloody murder and within days, if not hours, that "discriminatory" program would be shut down.

They'd whine about how Title VI of the Civil Rights Act prohibits discrimination based on race, color, or national origin, in any program supported by federal funds—which includes just about every college and university in the country.

Yet right now, more than 700 American colleges and universities openly violate Title VI by distributing scholarship aid to minority group members based on the race of the recipient.

Worse, the Department of Education (DOE) has said it will take no action against those colleges and universities that violate Title VI by offering race-based scholarships, despite its clear statutory obligation to do so.

That's why, in March, 1991, WLF filed suit in U.S. District Court for the District of Columbia against top DOE officials in an effort to force DOE to enforce federal civil rights laws against colleges and universities that provide financial aid on the basis of race.

WLF filed the lawsuit, *WLF v. Alexander,* on its own behalf and as counsel to seven students currently enrolled in colleges all across the country, students who have been denied access to financial aid on the basis of their race.

Students like Catherine Ficco of Mercy College in Dobbs Ferry, N.Y., who applied to the New York State Department of Education for a Regents Professional Opportunity Scholarship. They denied her request, saying she was ineligible even though she is economically disadvantaged—because she is not a member of a qualifying minority group.

And like Daniel Young, a law student at UCLA who was awarded a GAP grant by UCLA for the 1989-90 financial year. But, at registration, UCLA personnel saw Daniel wasn't black, said his GAP award had been a "mistake," and rescinded it.

Each student has a similar story. Each was discriminated against unfairly and illegally. And, with no one else seeming to care about *their* civil rights, they asked WLF for help.

It wasn't an easy decision for those youngsters. And the pressures placed upon them as a result have been tremendous. Some have been threatened. Others have been told their chances for a career have been ruined.

But none of those threats alter the facts one single bit: these students and others like them are victims of racial discrimination and sadly symptomatic of a steadily worsening national trend.

In Boston, for example, school district plans to lay off 500 of its 4,315 teachers ran into trouble when a federal judge ruled that, no matter what a seniority clause in the teachers' contracts says, the layoff must ignore seniority in favor of keeping racial percentages.

That means that someone who has been an outstanding teacher for 15 years or more could be laid off to make sure there was room for a lousy teacher who has been employed for a year—simply because that first teacher is white and the second is black.

WLF is also in another case in which a school district was told to rehire and give five years back pay to a black teacher, despite the fact that she was fired under state law after failing a competency exam five times.

The Foundation's first battle against race-based scholarships came when they filed a complaint with DOE about a scholarship program at Florida Atlantic University.

Those full-tuition scholarships were offered to *all* black students—regardless of academic qualifications and financial need.

In other words, the son of a black millionaire could apply and receive the scholarship, even though he might be a lousy student. But the son of poor white parents couldn't even apply, no matter how good a student he might be.

In WLF's complaint filed with DOE, they asked for a nationwide investigation of similar programs, naming the Universities of Florida and Nebraska as two other schools with race-based scholarship programs.

They thought they had been victorious in December, 1990, when Michael Williams, head of DOE's Civil Rights section, said race-based scholarships could not be offered by universities receiving federal funds.

But it proved to be an extremely short-lived victory. To put it mildly, the ultraliberals were outraged.

They mounted a pull-out-all-the-stops pressure campaign, like they used against Judge Bork, and less than a week after Williams had declared race-exclusive scholarships illegal, DOE caved in and said basically, "Keep doing business as usual."

WLF believed that Michael Williams' first decision was correct as a matter of law and that the new DOE policy was nothing more than the substitution of bad politics for good law.

And they believed that at a time when America needs desperately to train the best, to hire and depend on the best, programs and actions like these tend to shut the best out.

There's no question that many blacks and members of other minority groups come from economically deprived backgrounds. But they should receive scholarship aid based on their economic need, not on their skin color.

Unfortunately, America's education system is

very much controlled by ultraliberals who hesitate at nothing in order to impose their twisted view of the world on all Americans.

What other explanation is there for the fact that at Penn State black students get paid for even mediocre grades—$550 for a C to C+, $1,100 for anything better?

Or how else to explain why UCLA's political science department would advertise openings for minorities and women—no white males need apply?

This American trend would be bad enough, dangerous enough, if it were limited to education, but it's popping up everywhere.

And it needs to be addressed—quickly, before it splits this nation apart once again.

WLF v. Alexander seeks to address this critical issue. No decision had been reached as this book was prepared for publication.

Fighting the War Against Drugs

When William Bennett was named "Drug Czar," appointed to lead America's war against the proliferation and growing danger of illegal drugs, one of the first organizations he turned to for advice and assistance was the Washington Legal Foundation.

He said, "You have a unique perspective on the drug problem. As we develop our National Strategy, I would like to have your views, ideas and suggestions on hand to consider."

Bennett knew that WLF has consistently fought for tougher penalties for drug users and dealers and has also been in the forefront in the drive for mandatory drug testing, especially for individuals working in positions that could have a serious impact on the safety and well-being of other Americans.

WLF's involvement in the war against drugs has by no means been limited to courtroom actions.

Its voice was one of the first heard throughout the Washington bureaucracy advocating random drug testing for all federal employees in sensitive positions.

They have also been a regular voice in the regulatory arena, calling for drug testing of any employees involved in regulated activities when those employees could endanger lives or the public safety by functioning under the influence of drugs or alcohol.

National Treasury Employees Union v. Von Raab

WLF was an active and influential participant in the first case related to employee drug testing to be heard by the United States Supreme Court.

The case was made more interesting—and more challenging—for WLF by the involvement on the other side of not just such expected opponents as the ACLU, but also the powerful unions that represent many federal employees.

WLF General Counsel Dan Popeo is a big believer in drug testing and has been for years. While illegal drug use anywhere, by its very nature, is a criminal offense, he admits nothing can be done about what people do in the privacy of their own homes.

But he feels there is a great deal that can be done—and must be done—about people who place lives in danger every day by "trying to perform their jobs while they're stoned out of their minds on drugs."

He points to rail workers as a prime example, citing estimates by rail workers themselves that anywhere from 20% to 80% of their fellow workers report for duty under the influence of drugs or alcohol.

That's what leads directly to tragedies like the January, 1987, horror right outside Washington when an Amtrak passenger train hurtling down the track at 105 miles per hour plowed into three Conrail locomotives, killing 16 people and injuring more than 170 others.

Why did that crash occur? The Conrail engineer, who had been smoking marijuana, simply ignored several warning signals until it was too late for him to stop. He, of course, walked away from the carnage unhurt.

Then there are the air traffic controllers, people in enormously stress-filled jobs where one careless mistake can cost hundreds, perhaps even thousands, of lives.

Estimates are that as many as half of the controllers in some major airports carry out their functions under the influence of drugs or alcohol.

These people are responsible for guiding passenger-packed airplanes into and out of airports in the most heavily populated cities in America.

As Popeo told a group of WLF supporters,

Every time I hear a train going by my family's home, every time I hear an airplane flying overhead, my heart skips a beat, as I wonder about the people in charge. Are they drunk, have they been smoking marijuana, snorting cocaine, shooting heroin. Are they in control?

The experts agree that the best safeguard to prevent drug and alcohol abuse from destroying lives like that is a mandatory program of random drug testing for people engaged in those and similar activities.

Yet, when the Transportation Department instituted such mandatory testing for railroad workers who had been involved in accidents, a California federal appeals court ruled it was unconstitutional. And that case only dealt with testing *after* the fact, not with the issue of preventive testing in advance.

There seems to be a special irony in the fact that, in *National Treasury Employees Union v. Von Raab*, the ACLU and the Treasury Employees union were representing Customs Service employees, specifically those who are directly involved in drug-interdiction programs, who carry weapons, or who have access to classified information.

The U.S. Customs Service is America's first line of defense against the constant flow of illegal drugs into this country—and their employees union was fighting drug testing.

They said America doesn't have a right to make sure federal employees in key drug enforcement positions are not drug users themselves.

WLF, representing among others the Allied Educational Foundation, the National Federation of Parents for a Drug-Free Youth, and the Parents' Association to Neutralize Drug & Alcohol Abuse, argued that the public has the right to ensure that federal employees in the vanguard of our nation's war on drugs do not use the very drugs they are charged with intercepting.

The Foundation also argued that drug testing for such positions does not even implicate, let alone violate, the Fourth Amendment.

In the Supreme Court, the Justices agreed with WLF's position that there were no constitutional violations and allowed the Customs Service's drug testing program to stand.

Harmon v. Thornburgh

In another case, the Justice Department under President Reagan instituted a random drug testing program for employees in certain key positions.

WLF had been urging the use of random drug testing in the Justice Department and other sensitive federal agencies since 1981, even before President Reagan made it a priority of his administration.

In the Justice Department case, 42 department attorneys and other employees represented by the ACLU brought suit, seeking to enjoin the testing program.

Of special note in this case, in which WLF actively participated, was the fact that the Justice Department, in papers it filed to seek summary judgment in the lower court, had reproduced WLF's brief in the Supreme Court case, *National Treasury Employees Union v. Von Raab,* as a supporting exhibit.

In a victory for public safety, the U.S. Court of Appeals for the District of Columbia upheld the use of random drug testing for those DOJ employees with top security clearances and for those employees with regular access to classified information or standby clearance.

The victory, however, was not complete. The court did enjoin the remainder of the DOJ drug testing program which required testing of prosecutors in criminal cases and employees with access to grand jury proceedings.

However, the court also indicated that random drug testing of drug prosecutors might withstand constitutional scrutiny.

In a subsequent case, *Willner v. Thornburgh,* in which WLF was again involved on the side of the Justice Department, the U.S. Court of Appeals for the District of Columbia Circuit ruled that the Justice Department could administer drug tests to attorneys who are seeking employment with the department.

The Court ruled that job applicants have a lesser expectation of privacy than do employees and that the government had a sufficiently important interest which justified that minimal intrusion on the applicants' privacy.

In WLF's brief supporting the Department's drug testing program, the Foundation argued that such testing does not violate the Fourth Amendment rights of job applicants to be free from unreasonable searches and seizures, and that drug testing is the only effective means of ensuring that the prospective employees are not habitual drug users.

As the book went to press, the Court of Appeals was considering a re-hearing of this case.

Support for Tougher, Mandatory Sentencing

When Ronald Harmelin was arrested in Oak Park, Michigan, he was a one-man drug market.

Police found on his person: marijuana cigarettes, brass cocaine straws, a cocaine spoon, three vials of cocaine, over 3 dozen narcotics pills, a .38 caliber revolver, a beeper, nearly $600 in cash—in other words, all the tools of his trade.

And that was just on his person. In his car they found nearly $3,000 in cash, plus a pound and a half of pure cocaine with a street value of as much as $100,000.

He was convicted and, as required under Michigan law, was given the mandatory sentence for possession of more than 650 grams of cocaine—life in prison without the possibility of parole.

The Court of Appeals upheld both his conviction and his sentence, and the State Supreme Court denied his request for review.

But then the ACLU came along, howling that

Ronald Harmelin's sentence of life without parole constitutes "cruel and unusual punishment."

As Dan Popeo noted, the "ACLU doesn't think we should punish drug dealers. They think they should be allowed to sell their poison to anyone who wants it, young or old, rich or poor!"

"Who cares about 'crack' babies? Who cares that most of the murders and violent crimes in this country are drug-related? Who cares about an entire generation of young people with their lives at risk?"

The ACLU somehow convinced the Supreme Court to hear Harmelin's case on the basis that his sentence did violate the Eighth Amendment's prohibition against cruel and unusual punishment.

WLF, representing among others, Citizens for Law and Order, Families and Friends of Missing Persons and Violent Crimes Victims, the Maryland Coalition Against Crime, the Parents Association to Neutralize Drug and Alcohol Abuse, and the Stephanie Roper Committee, argued that Harmelin's sentence is not disproportionate to his crime in light of the tremendous harm inflicted on society by drug traffickers.

As this was written, the Supreme Court, having heard oral arguments in this case, was deliberating, and a decision was anticipated at any time.

What Side of the Drug War Are These Judges On?

By now there's not an American alive who doesn't know that our nation is in a war against drugs. A very dangerous, deadly war.

That's because this war is being waged in cities and towns all across America and, judging from the headlines and the news reports of ride-by shootings, gang wars, street corner executions, plus the ever increasing rate of burglaries and armed robberies to help pay for more drugs, it's a war that honest, mainstream Americans are in danger of losing.

But the war on drugs is being fought in other arenas, too, notably the nation's courtrooms. And the way a number of judges treat drug pushers, America is losing the war on that front, too.

Imagine being a policeman or representative of some other law enforcement agency. You risk your life to gather the necessary evidence to arrest a major drug kingpin and bring him to trial.

The evidence is sound, the case strong—but the judge just lets him go, turns him back onto the streets so he can resume his dangerous criminal activity.

It's disgusting, it's disgraceful, but it happens day in and day out in courtrooms all across the country.

The following stories tell of three different judges and their approach to America's drug wars. Unfortunately, it's all too easy to see exactly which side each of these men is on.

Judge Robert W. Sweet

"Cocaine gives a sense of exhilaration, heroin a glow, a warmth, and marijuana a sense of relaxation and ease. What then is wrong?"

The words could come from a mail-order catalogue of illegal drugs, or at least from the smooth, polished sales pitch of a street corner pusher.

But that's not where these words came from. They're right from the mouth of New York federal judge Robert W. Sweet, uttered in a public speech advocating the legalization of these and other drugs.

Heroin, cocaine, crack, marijuana, angel dust—this active, sitting federal judge whose caseload is filled with drug trials, would make them all legal.

This Carter-appointed liberal took his pro-drug stand in a speech to his wife's women's club but, concerned that there might not be enough media coverage, took the precautionary step of circulating copies of his speech beforehand to the national media.

Then, just to make sure no one missed out on what he was promoting, he took his legalization message on the talk show circuit.

In doing so, Judge Sweet became the first federal official in any branch of government to call for the legalization of harmful drugs which have been declared illegal by America's elected representatives, both in the Congress and in all 50 states and the District of Columbia.

Rather than showing concern for lives destroyed by drugs, rather than caring about the brutal crimes that drug users commit to pay for their drugs or their even more violent actions after using them, Judge

Sweet instead says, "I suggest it is time . . . to cease treating indulgence in mind alteration as a crime."

As Washington Legal Foundation Executive Legal Director Paul Kamenar suggested during this episode, for Judge Sweet "to say that drugs are simply mind-altering is mind-boggling. Maybe he should start his education by talking to the doctors and nurses who take care of more than 200,000 crack-addicted babies."

Judge Sweet destroyed forever any lingering image of being an impartial jurist. Like too many other ultraliberal members of the judiciary, he lost sight of the fact that his job is to enforce laws, not to make them.

Sweet was still making the rounds of the talk shows when WLF filed its Complaint of Judicial Misconduct, calling for his immediate removal from the bench, or at the very least, barring him from hearing any future drug cases.

Unfortunately, his colleagues chose to protect him and dismissed WLF's complaint. Still, the Foundation received some good news shortly after that when Judge Sweet went into semi-retirement.

Judge Donald A. Smith

On the surface, this appeared to be a fairly simple case, very cut and dried. And it certainly should have been.

James Hennessey had one of the most sensitive jobs in a major New Jersey oil refinery, directing the flow of hundreds of thousands of gallons of highly-inflammable crude oil.

Then, under the company's safety-based random drug testing program, he tested positive for both marijuana and valium.

Here was someone manning critical controls where one slip, one mistake could lead to a major disaster costing hundreds, maybe even thousands of lives—and he's high on drugs.

The company was vastly relieved to find out about Hennessey's drug use before such a disaster, rather than after, especially since the discovery came close on the heels of a major refinery explosion in Houston.

So they fired him. Which should have been the end of the story.

But it wasn't. Hennessey was taken under the protective hand of the ACLU. Screaming "violation of constitutional rights," they helped him file suit against his employer to get his job back.

Hennessey v. Coastal Eagle Point Oil Company was argued before Superior Court Judge Donald A. Smith.

Citing other New Jersey cases which had limited the ability of *public* sector employers to test their employees for drug use, Smith in an absurd abuse of logic "reasoned" that it must be public policy in New Jersey not to do drug testing.

Not only did this man order that Hennessey be given his extremely sensitive job back, endangering the lives of anyone who lived near the refinery, not to mention those who worked there—but he ordered the company to pay damages to Smith in the amount of $100,000!

As WLF General Counsel Dan Popeo' commented at the time, "Wow! Just think how much marijuana the guy can buy with that kind of money.

Lives endangered, public safety threatened? So what! That's not nearly as important as a pothead's right to get stoned on the job if he wants to. At least in Judge Smith's twisted view of the law."

Of course, the dangers in that warped decision go beyond the immediate danger posed by returning Hennessey to his job.

By imposing public-sector policy on the private sector, Judge Smith tried to tie the hands of private industry and to eliminate the use of preventive drug measures even for employees whose duties directly affect the safety of our families.

While the ACLU continued to represent Hennessey, WLF immediately entered the case to help Hennessey's employer in appealing Judge Smith's decision.

In April, 1991, the New Jersey Superior Court Appellate Division sided with WLF and overturned the lower court decision, ruling that a private employer can indeed conduct random drug tests of employees.

Judge Stanley Klavan

Perhaps no judge's stand on drugs caused greater aggravation at Washington Legal Foundation than the actions of Judge Stanley Klavan.

The judge presided over a Maryland case involving an eviction from a public housing project. There had been a steady stream of complaints about a particular unit, traffic in and out of the place at all hours, loud arguments and music, drug paraphernalia all over the place, and much more.

At one time used syringes had been found in a

place where children could be hurt by them. Razor blades used to "cut" cocaine were also found.

On more than one occasion, the police came in search of regular visitors who were believed to be involved with the use or sale of illegal drugs and other dangerous substances.

When police arrived on the scene with a search warrant, no one seemed at all surprised when they found a bag with at least 15 rocks of "crack" and several items of drug paraphernalia.

The police arrested three residents of the housing unit, charging them with maintaining a common nuisance, possession of controlled dangerous substances with intent to distribute, and possession of cocaine.

Then, armed with the complaints and with the evidence obtained by the police, the Housing Opportunities Commission (HOC) sent a notice of eviction to the tenant in an effort to restore peace and safety for her neighbors.

Not wanting to be bothered with having to move, however, or to have to set up a new location to do her illegal business, the tenant hired an ACLU-type lawyer to fight the eviction.

To the amazement of almost everyone, when the case was heard by Judge Klavan, he ruled the eviction invalid, thereby allowing the tenant to continue her criminal activity in her tax-supported residence.

To make matters worse, during the trial, Judge Klavan engaged in a dialogue with the tenant's attorney in a manner that actually helped him argue his case. Then Judge Klavan turned around and accused the HOC's attorney of hysteria.

In fact, he went far beyond even that. Here's part of what Judge Klavan had to say about this case and about the matter of drug use in America in general.

> *Let's not get hysterical about this. . . . you have proven . . . that she had an old bong and she has some razor blades in the house, razor blades are always in houses and with a police officer everything becomes an implement of narcotics these days. . . . if you want to take a shave, you better be careful, you might be found to be violating the controlled substance law.*

Then Judge Klavan expanded his sphere and accused the "whole country" of . . .

> *. . . becoming hysterical over what they say is the drug problem (when) they ought to become more hysterical over the problem of the ghettos . . . The real problem is the fact that we have the fourth world living in this country, the world of the under class, and if they do not get that problem taken care of, this won't even be a problem.*

Near the conclusion of his decision, Judge Klavan came back to his hysteria theme once again when he said, "There is a lot of hysteria in this country and it is uncalled for."

In Dan Popeo's eyes, judges like Stanley Klavan are as dangerous as the drug dealers and users they support.

He asked, "How can he blatantly ignore the fact that 3 out of every 4 robberies, muggings, burglaries, and similar crimes in this country today are drug related?

"And, if he is so concerned about the problems of the poor, how can he blatantly trample on the rights of other residents of this complex to live in peace and safety?"

Even as they began working with the Housing Opportunities Commission to get Judge Klavan's decision overturned, WLF also took immediate steps against the judge as well.

Circulating a Petition to Support a Complaint of Judicial Misconduct among WLF's supporters and amassing thousands of signed petitions, WLF filed a Complaint of Judicial Misconduct against Judge Klavan with the Commission on Judicial Disabilities.

Through its nationwide Court Watch program, WLF continues to monitor the activities of any and all judges whose track record seems grossly inconsistent with the laws they have sworn to uphold.

Judges Need to Be Reminded of Role in America's Justice System

In many ways, it seems America is the victim of an out-of-control judiciary.

As our elected representatives in Congress seem more and more to wallow in the comfort of guaranteed re-election and a seemingly unending string of scandals, the judiciary has assumed a greater and greater role in our country's management, and in our destiny.

Judges who are appointed to interpret and apply the law increasingly take it upon themselves to "make" the law as well.

All the laws in the land are meaningless if judges do not apply them the way they were meant to be applied.

Every time a violent criminal is turned back onto the streets, every time a judge overrules decisions made by a voting public, every time a judge forces his or her own twisted agenda on to the American people, we are seeing an out-of-control judiciary.

And in many ways, America's renowned system of checks and balances falls short when confronted with a power-hungry judiciary.

Whereas we are quick to prosecute and control members of the executive and legislative branches of our government who stray beyond the boundaries of their responsibilities, it is much more difficult to hold judges accountable either for their excesses or for their inadequacies.

The Radical Left legal groups would not have been able to assume the degree of control they have held over America's court system for decades without the willing acquiescence, if not support, of the judges who ruled on their anti-American lawsuits.

Whether it's turning criminals back out onto the streets or whether it's working hand in glove with the Radical Left to force unwelcome and unwarranted actions on to the American people, our judicial system needs to be restored to one that serves those people, not one that ignores or abuses them.

This chapter examines decisions and behavior by judges that flies in the face of the public trust they are given and which they have sworn to uphold.

Sympathy for the Rapist

There are parts of this story that are extremely difficult to believe. It's all true.

It happened in New Mexico.

A young mother named Lisa, who was 22 but was described as looking more like 16, was kidnapped by a cab driver, Richard Neal.

Neal kept Lisa captive in his apartment while repeatedly beating her and subjecting her to sexual assault.

After two weeks of that treatment, unable to take food or drink, Lisa died of malnutrition.

When she died, Neal calmly loaded her lifeless but still warm body into his cab and drove to a nearby parking lot. There he coldheartedly dumped his victim's body and drove off.

In the two weeks Neal held Lisa captive, she lost 25 pounds. An autopsy found bruises on her jaw, her chest and her arms, probably caused by blows from a fist.

Her condition was so bad it took more than a week for her body to be identified—and even then it took dental records to be sure.

When her sister saw Lisa's body, she could barely recognize her, saying that her features were "withered" and "shrunken" and that she looked to be 30 years older.

Neal had been fully aware of what he was doing. He had seen news reports of Lisa's disappearance. He simply chose to ignore them and in fact even boasted to his fellow cabbies about having sex with a "retarded" girl who was "staying" with him.

One cabdriver who saw Lisa in Neal's apartment was concerned by her poor condition and urged Neal to get her to a doctor. The next day, Neal told him that he had taken Lisa to the hospital and that her parents had come to take her home. All the while, she remained his captive, starving in his apartment.

When Neal was later arrested by police, he pled no contest to charges of involuntary manslaughter, false imprisonment, and two counts of criminal assault.

Yet despite an overwhelming array of evidence, despite Neal's "no contest" plea, despite Lisa's tragic and painful death, and despite the prosecutor's plea for a stiff prison sentence, Judge Albert Murdoch, citing "sympathy" he felt for the rapist, said he "could not see any act of malice on Neal's part," sentenced him only to the time he had already spent in jail, releasing him onto the streets.

By now it should come as a surprise to no one,

including Judge Murdoch, that Neal repeated his crime.

Only this time, the victim of his sexual molestation was a four-year-old girl!

Four years old and already this little girl is bearing scars that may never completely heal. And her family shares those scars and that burden with their daughter.

All thanks to a judge who felt "sympathy" for an admitted rapist.

If only judges like Albert Murdoch felt even a little of the pity for the victim that they feel for the criminal, America's courts would be a much fairer place, would be far more just!

Sadly, but again not surprisingly, this was not the first time Judge Murdoch had been lenient on a violent criminal.

But WLF, representing Lisa's family, did everything in its power to make certain it was his last.

Immediately upon learning the facts of this travesty of justice, WLF filed a formal complaint with the New Mexico Judicial Standards Commission, charging Judge Murdoch with willful misconduct and violations of the canons of Judicial Ethics.

The pressure had an immediate impact. When Neal re-appeared before Murdoch for the sexual molestation of that little girl, the judge was forced to impose the maximum possible sentence on Neal— because he knew the whole world was watching.

And that same pressure will hang over Judge Murdoch's head—unless WLF is instrumental in having him removed from the bench—for each and every criminal case he tries.

Taxation without Representation

It's an issue that launched a revolution more than 200 years ago.

And our Founding Fathers, when they drafted the Constitution, knew that even in the right hands, the power to tax is dangerous, so they left no doubt at all as to where that power was to reside—in the legislative branch of the American government.

Not in the presidency, not in the hands of federal judges, but in the hands of our elected representatives.

Unfortunately, in this and other matters, certain judges continue to envision themselves as above both the law and the Constitution.

The residents of Kansas City found that out when U.S. District Judge Russell G. Clark, by court order, threw the Constitution into the wastebasket and gave himself the power to impose taxes.

Another of Jimmy Carter's infamous appointees, Judge Clark ordered residents of the Kansas City School District to ante up additional taxes to help pay for $285 million in "improvements" to that city's schools—improvements which were decided upon by none other than Judge Clark himself.

To make this bizarre story even worse, Kansas City's schools were already AAA-rated by the State of Missouri, their highest rating. And the school district already allotted more than $4,000 per pupil, one of the highest sums per student of any district in the state.

Nonetheless, Judge Clark felt that those schools weren't integrated enough and, in the classic liberal tradition, decided he could solve that problem the same way you solve any other problem—throw money at it.

In this case the money he decided to throw was $285 million. Yes, that's a lot of money, but that didn't worry Judge Clark. He knew where to get it—from the pockets of the hard-working citizens of Kansas City, rich and poor, black and white.

He simply increased those citizens' state income taxes by 25% and nearly doubled their property tax.

And what were these over-taxed citizens to get for all that money? It seems Judge Clark has some rather unusual ideas of ways to promote desegregation in a school system.

Among the "improvements" he ordered were:

A log cabin with heat, lights, and toilets for environmental studies.

A 25-acre working farm with a barn and an apartment for a caretaker.

A 1,875 square-foot school "animal room"—a space that Missouri's governor described as "larger than most Missouri family homes."

At one school, a swimming complex, with Olympic-sized pool and seating for 400, plus a spa and a soccer field separate from the regular football field.

Judge Clark ordered those absurd "improvements," despite the fact that the State of Missouri had already been forced to spend over $330 million on previous desegregation orders.

According to the Governor, that would have been enough money to: give every classroom teacher in the state a $5,000 bonus; increase minimum teacher salaries to $21,000; pay a full semester's tuition and fees for every student at Missouri's four-year public colleges and universities; and still have some $20 million left over.

The citizens of Kansas City had voted year after year against any tax increases. But to judges like Russell Clark, it doesn't matter what the voters decide on, he'll just do what he wants to do anyway.

It was Missouri's Republican U.S. Senator John Danforth and two Missouri State Representatives who asked WLF to represent them in a legal effort to oppose and overturn Judge Clark's insidious, illegal order.

WLF filed a brief in the Eighth Circuit, challenging Judge Clark's order, arguing that such court-ordered taxation violates the principles of federalism and separation of powers as provided for in the Constitution.

The case eventually reached the U.S. Supreme Court where the justices ruled that Judge Clark could not raise income taxes as part of his efforts at "remedying" the desegregation "problem" in Kansas City's schools.

Head in the Sand

From Kansas City to Yonkers.

Sometimes it seems as if these federal judges are trying to outdo one another in the sheer outrageousness of their actions.

In Yonkers, New York, another judge took it upon himself to go way beyond the bounds of his office in order to see that his own personal desegregation wishes were carried out.

He's Federal District Judge Leonard B. Sand,

whose name has become synonymous (since the day he was appointed by Jimmy Carter) with wild-eyed ultraliberal decisions from his bench.

Spallone v. United States came about after Judge Sand had ordered the construction of some 1,000 units of public housing to help remedy an alleged "pattern and practice" of racial discrimination.

However, the taxpaying citizens of Yonkers objected vehemently to this housing project proposed to be built in their midst. And, in fine and proper American tradition, they made their objections known to those who represented them, their elected officials, in this case the members of the Yonkers City Council.

Well, those Council members saw it as their obligation to represent the wishes of the people who had elected them, so four of the Council members simply refused to vote for an ordinance that would put the court-ordered agreement into effect.

To put it mildly, Judge Sand went ballistic. In a raw exercise of power that went far beyond the proper limits of his office, he said, "This court will tolerate no further violation of its lawful orders."

He ordered the hesitant Councilmen to vote for the housing ordinance, and he forbade them to resign from City Council in order to avoid having to vote for his ordinance.

Furthermore, to make absolutely certain his orders were carried out this time, he ordered that "each of the Council members who fails to vote in favor of the enactment of such legislation shall be personally fined $500 per day."

That was on July 26. Still not content, however,

he added that if they had still not carried out his order by August 10, the Council members "shall be committed to the United States marshal for imprisonment."

In addition, the city itself was ordered to pay a fine starting at $100 a day and doubling every day until the ordinance was passed.

The City of Yonkers wound up paying $820,000 in fines, and each of the defiant Councilmen paid $3,500.

As syndicated columnist James Kilpatrick wrote, "What are the limits of judicial power? In the Yonkers case, an unelected federal judge usurped the power of lawfully elected city councilmen. The judge reduced them to puppets dangling from judicial strings."

City Councilman Henry G. Spallone appealed Judge Sand's flagrant abuse of judicial power. WLF joined in the case, representing the Save Yonkers Federation (as they had several years earlier in the discrimination suit that was the underlying basis for *Spallone*).

WLF argued that the principles of federalism and separation of powers forbid a federal judge from using the contempt power to force democratically elected legislators to pass laws of the judge's choosing.

On January 10, 1990, the Supreme Court agreed with WLF's arguments and announced its decision overturning the fines Judge Sand had imposed on the Yonkers Council members.

A Kick for Judge O'Kicki

Shortly before work began on this book, WLF was asked for help by a group of taxpayers in Pennsylvania.

These taxpayers resented vehemently the fact that their tax dollars were being used to pay the $80,000 annual salary for a judge who had been charged and convicted of six counts of public corruption and sentenced to two to five years in prison.

Judge Joseph O'Kicki was a judge on the Pennsylvania Court of Common Pleas in Johnstown. Back in 1988 he had been charged by a grand jury with misconduct and suspended with pay.

A year later came the convictions and prison sentence.

Yet this corrupt judge who got caught still did not pay the price.

The Administrative Office of the Pennsylvania Courts (AOPC) continued paying Judge O'Kicki's salary in clear violation of the state constitution which provides that a judge is "automatically" removed from office upon "conviction for misbehavior in office." Payments were still being made a year and a half after the conviction.

Apparently Judge O'Kicki felt he was above the law when he committed his crimes and still felt he was above the law even after he had been convicted.

In *WLF v. O'Kicki*, Washington Legal Foundation attorneys filed suit on behalf of those Pennsylvania taxpayers against the head of the AOPC in Pennsylvania's Commonwealth Court, demanding an immediate injunction against further payments of O'Kicki's "salary."

Since the AOPC is a Pennsylvania state agency, it could have been expected that the state attorney general would defend the suit on behalf of AOPC. Instead, shortly after WLF filed the suit, the attorney general held a press conference in which he said that all further payments to O'Kicki should cease.

He also sent a letter to the Pennsylvania State Treasurer stating that if the payments were not stopped, he would contemplate filing a lawsuit of his own.

This case, which should have never been necessary in the first place, at least ended in victory when the Pennsylvania State Supreme Court ruled that payments to O'Kicki should cease immediately.

Dethroning the "King"

WLF is, as of this writing, deeply involved in a case in Dallas, Texas, an extremely flagrant example of a federal judge showing total disregard for the law and for ethical standards of behavior.

The judge in question is U.S. District Court Judge Jerry Buchmeyer. Dan Popeo described Judge Buchmeyer to WLF's supporters as a "Jimmy Carter-appointed liberal, and to call his behavior simply inappropriate would be like calling Saddam Hussein a benevolent dictator."

Referred to as "King Jerry I," Buchmeyer was caught by WLF in major violations of the Judicial Code of Conduct for his handling of a voting rights case—and the cover-up he undertook when WLF blew the whistle on him.

It seems that, in a lawsuit filed against the City of Dallas, activists claimed that because too few minority group members were elected to the City Council, the entire election process violated federal voting rights laws and should therefore be thrown out.

Those activists were delighted with the news that Judge "King Jerry" Buchmeyer had been assigned to the case. Their delight was justified when he decreed that voting discrimination had occurred because "African-Americans and Hispanics cannot raise enough money to run an effective campaign" for some of the City Council seats.

So, with that marvelous logic, King Jerry throws out Dallas' election process. To carry out his decree, the City scheduled a referendum. It didn't take long for it to become clear that the voters were not going to sit idly by and let King Jerry's plan be rammed down their throats.

A worried Dallas Mayor, Annette Strauss, telephoned the judge directly and asked him what he would do if the voters were to reject the plan. With the blessing of the activists' lawyers, King Jerry told her that he would impose the plan anyway by judicial fiat; it didn't matter what the voters wanted.

He also told her not to tell anyone they talked, to lie if necessary. He also didn't bother to get permission from the city attorneys to have this secret talk with the Mayor.

When WLF first learned of Buchmeyer's actions, representing Tom Pauken of Dallas who headed up the successful citizens campaign to defeat the referendum, they filed a formal Judicial Misconduct Complaint with the Judicial Council of the Fifth

Circuit against Judge Buchmeyer's handling of the case and for having secret talks with the Mayor without prior approval from the city's attorneys, clear violations of the Code of Judicial Conduct.

Buchmeyer formally answered the WLF complaint, flatly denying the charges, and claimed he did in fact get permission from the City Attorney to talk with the Mayor.

He was reprimanded only for having an "ill-advised" conversation with the Mayor. As Dan Popeo told WLF supporters, "'Ill-advised?' How about coverup, obstruction of justice, abuse of judicial powers, lying to higher court officers. It's all here and we're going to prove it."

Unbeknownst to Buchmeyer, the City Attorney and the Mayor had already filed sworn affidavits denying that the judge had contacted the City's attorneys and disputing the judge's version of the events.

Armed with those signed affidavits and additional proof of his crimes, WLF filed a second set of misconduct charges against the judge for his deceitful response to the initial charges.

Representing Pauken as well as Dallas City Councilmen Glenn Box and Jerry Bartos, WLF demanded at a minimum that Judge Buchmeyer be removed not just from the case in question but from every case involving the City of Dallas.

There were 13 such cases on the books at the time, and WLF argued that it would be impossible for the city to get fair and impartial treatment in any of them.

In addition, however, they also wanted Judge Buchmeyer removed from the bench, seeing him as just another example of radical judges teaming up with ultraliberal legal groups to undermine the voting power and rights of the American people.

So they hope to use Judge Buchmeyer's case to send a message into courtrooms all across America, according to Popeo: "No more backroom deals with civil rights plaintiffs, no more cases decided before the first shred of evidence is introduced, no more lies and coverups."

Incredibly, Circuit Judge Politz, another Carter-appointee, dismissed WLF's second complaint without mentioning one word about the cover-up and lies!

As this was written, WLF was preparing an appeal to the full Fifth Circuit Judicial Council.

Time to Bar the Bar Association

Perhaps no single case in the history of the Washington Legal Foundation was more important, harder fought, or drew more nationwide attention than its lawsuit against the American Bar Association's illegal influence over the selection and appointment of federal judges.

This case, which went on for four years before being decided in the U.S. Supreme Court, also marked perhaps the only time in memory that Ralph Nader and Dan Popeo have been on the same side of an issue.

Since 1948, the ABA's Standing Committee on the Federal Judiciary had served as an advisory group to the Senate Judiciary Committee, a sort of clearing-house for nominees and potential nominees to federal judgeships. Their guidelines called for the committee to rate the "competence, integrity and judicial temperament" of prospective nominees.

On the surface, it sounds respectable enough, and that may well be how it was in the early years, an impartial committee of distinguished lawyers whose objectivity would help offset the political aspects of some judicial appointments.

Over those years, however, the effective role of the committee turned a complete 180 degrees.

Plus, the committee's power had grown to the extent that when the President of the United States would submit to the ABA committee for their approval or disapproval the names of individuals he was considering for such appointment, a disapproval or "negative" rating had become the equivalent of a total veto, effectively killing the nomination right on the spot.

Worse, the ABA's Standing Committee on the Federal Judiciary was so packed with liberal activist lawyers that it looked to conservative judicial nominees more like the Inquisition than like a simple, fact-finding evaluation.

Fed up with President Reagan's inability to gain approval for several conservative choices for federal judge positions, WLF launched an extensive investigation into the ABA committee's practices and amassed a considerable body of evidence to support the fact that approval or disapproval was determined not by a nominee's abilities or qualifications but by the nominee's perceived ideological position.

Simply put, a nominee whose ideology or personal beliefs did not conform to the ABA's own left-wing political agenda was not very likely to receive approval.

Some of the more blatant examples include:

As Chairman of the taxpayer-supported Legal Services Corporation, Professor William Harvey eliminated $400,000 in public funding to the ABA's activist attorney groups. When he was nominated for a federal judgeship, he received a negative rating.

Lino Graglia is a nationally-renowned constitutional law professor at the University of Texas with flawless credentials. The ABA rejected his nomination because he opposes forced school busing, a pet liberal program.

> *At the time of his nomination, James Graham was a member of the American College of Trial Lawyers, chairman of the Ohio Board of Examiners, a respected lawyer with more than 24 years of litigation experience. Graham was given low ratings by the ABA—because he was a practicing Christian.*

Of course, opposition to conservative judicial nominees by ultraliberals reached a fever pitch when President Reagan nominated Robert Bork to the Supreme Court.

Obviously unable to go after Bork's impeccable credentials, the liberal forces instead unleashed a scathing attack against the man for his refusal to be a judicial activist, for believing that the proper role of a judge is to interpret law, not make law.

Ted Kennedy's sickening tirade against Judge Bork will live as one of the most disgusting assaults on a person's character and a blatant effort to inflame emotions with absolutely no regard for the truth.

Kennedy, a person of such high moral standards himself, described Robert Bork's America as

> *a land in which women would be forced into back-alley abortions, blacks would sit at segregated lunch counters, rogue police could break down citizens' doors in midnight raids, schoolchildren could not be taught about evolution, writers and artists could be censored at the whim of government, and the doors of the federal courts would be shut on the fingers of millions of citizens.*

But the greatest disgrace of all came when, in the course of its investigation, WLF learned that, in addition to the built-in bias of the Standing Committee on the Federal Judiciary, that committee had a practice of routinely inviting left-wing activist groups to review the President's recommendations for judicial appointments.

While mainstream Americans were placing their faith in our country's unique system of separation of powers and checks and balances, the truth of the matter was that groups like the ACLU, Norman Lear and his Hollywood-funded People for the American Way, the NAACP Legal Defense Fund, NOW, Common Cause, and others had virtual veto power over federal judicial nominations.

One of the groups involved in this mess was the Alliance for Justice's Judicial Selection Project, an ultra left-wing organization that exists for the sole purpose of preventing the appointment of conservatives to judgeships. Yet the ABA readily opened its files to them for their "help and advice" on potential judges.

Seeking a way to at least level the playing field, WLF in 1985 requested that the ABA Committee give the names of the judicial candidates to WLF for "help and advice" on the same basis as the liberal groups in order to provide some balance in the process.

The committee not only denied WLF's request but, caught with their hand in the cookie jar, tried to weasel out by proclaiming that, rather than have conservative input in the approval process, "the standing committee has concluded that a practice of furnishing lists of prospective nominees to organized groups is inconsistent with its concerns for confidentiality and obligations to the president."

That lofty statement left the door open wide, however, to some of the *individuals* who represent those groups, many of whom the standing committee continued to involve in the process—at least the liberal ones. WLF General Counsel Dan Popeo was still not on the committee's list of advisors.

Fed up, WLF filed a lawsuit in federal court in Washington against the ABA and its Standing Committee on the Federal Judiciary. The suit charged a violation of federal law, specifically a blatant violation of the Federal Advisory Committee Act of 1972 (FACA), which governs the procedures of those committees providing recommendations or advice to government officials.

FACA requires that all meetings, records, and minutes of such committees be open to the public, and further requires that the members of such advisory committees be fairly balanced in their viewpoints.

U.S. District Court Judge Joyce Hens Green handed WLF a partial victory in its lawsuit when she ruled that the ABA committee is a federal advisory committee. Unfortunately, she also immediately granted the committee a special exemption.

She ruled that to apply FACA to the committee's advisory proceedings would unconstitutionally interfere with the President's power to appoint federal judges! But it was the ABA that was really interfering.

Unsatisfied, WLF took its lawsuit to the U.S. Supreme Court.

It was during the Supreme Court's deliberations that WLF lost the battle but won the war. A sharply divided court decided that the ABA committee is not "utilized" by the Justice Department for advice or recommendations on the qualifications of candidates for the federal judiciary and is therefore not covered by FACA.

However, as a result of WLF's efforts and the national spotlight focused on the ABA committee's practices, the ABA agreed to discontinue the practices that WLF had objected to and, most important, included a commitment to end the practice of considering a judicial candidate's political or religious beliefs in its evaluations.

Also, to help see that those "commitments" are kept, Attorney General Richard Thornburgh and the Senate Judiciary Committee conditioned their continued use of ABA advice and recommendations on the implementation of the reforms that WLF had urged.

ABA: Money Launderers?

WLF's lawsuit against the American Bar Association's Standing Committee on the Federal Judiciary is certainly not the Foundation's only run-in with the ABA, far from it.

As Dan Popeo has noted,

> *Justice Department officials call it the Defendants Bar Association. I call it the Criminals Protective Association.*
>
> *Whatever you call it, the American Bar Association today is nothing more than a tool used by those who defend drug dealers, murderers, rapists, and pornographers, to keep their clients free while*

endangering the lives of every decent, honest American!

I'm sick and tired of their claims to be an objective professional organization when in truth they are nothing but an increasingly radical special interest group for the Left!

The occasion for those remarks was WLF's involvement against the ABA once again, this time in the case, *United States v. Fischetti, Pomerantz & Russo*.

The case focused on lawyers and their willingness to help drug dealers "launder" the money they make from their illegal activities. Although the law clearly prohibits this practice, too many lawyers, as is the case with too many judges, simply consider themselves somehow to be above the law.

The law in this case was one passed in 1984 which required anyone receiving $10,000 or more in cash in one or more related business transactions to report the name, address, and social security number of the person who paid the cash.

The reasons behind the law are reasonably obvious and certainly sound. Not only does it help track large sums of money for tax purposes, it also helps short-circuit the money laundering process drug dealers use to legitimize the massive amounts of illegal cash they take in.

In other words, it's not just a weapon for the tax collectors, it's a very badly needed weapon in the war against America's deadly drug trade.

The law applied to everyone. It listed no exemptions.

Lawyers, however, began complaining right

from the outset. Not all lawyers, just those with the kind of clients who are most apt to make cash payments of $10,000 or more.

They said it was a violation of attorney-client privilege and, since they consider themselves above the law anyway, simply refused to comply with the reporting requirement.

It was against that backdrop that *U.S. v. Fischetti* came about.

Two lawyers from a New York city firm which regularly represents drug dealers reported that five of their clients had made cash payments in excess of $10,000, but they refused to identify those clients.

So the government took them to court. And the government won a major victory when U.S. District Court Judge Vincent Broderick ordered the lawyers to turn over the requested information.

The lawyers in question, however, remained determined to protect their extremely lucrative clients who paid in cash, and filed for an immediate appeal.

It was when they did that the ABA jumped into this case on their side.

They filed a brief with the Court of Appeals that rambled on for 25 pages using all sorts of imaginative descriptions of the impact of this ruling on attorney-client privilege and other transactions.

WLF General Counsel Dan Popeo conceded the fact that a lawyer, "even one who regularly represents scum clients like drug dealers, has an obligation to represent his client to the best of his ability."

He added:

> *But never has attorney-client privilege been considered absolute. For example, a lawyer is obli-*

gated to report to authorities if he knows his client is about to commit a crime.

Above and beyond that, however, nowhere in its brief does the ABA address one simple, commonsense question—why don't the lawyers just ask their clients to put the money in a bank and write a check?

Obviously only someone with something to hide would object to the disclosure of his cash payments, and it should be equally obvious that a lawyer who accepts massive sums of cash without reporting it is engaging in money laundering.

Some 15,000 lawyers in this country have reported receiving $10,000 or more in cash payments but have refused to provide the information required to the IRS.

Even if each lawyer received no more than $10,000, that still amounts to $150 million—almost without question, every bit of it from illegal activities—that lawyers in this country are helping to launder.

The real number is almost certainly somewhere in the billions.

WLF, because of its long-standing interest in helping America win its war against drugs, was involved in this case before the ABA jumped in on the other side. They consider it a landmark case, a test of the government's right to use this important weapon in its war against the drug trade that threatens our entire nation.

But Dan Popeo also admits they consider it a test of just how powerful the American Bar Association is in our country today. He compared the ABA to a cancer growing on America that must be cut out if America is to survive.

On June 7, 1991, the Court of Appeals unanimously ruled in WLF's favor. The court stated that "the importance of client identification as a means of uncovering tax evasion is apparent" and brushed off the ABA's constitutional objection as "without merit."

The criminal defense lawyers have vowed to take this case to the Supreme Court; if they do, WLF has vowed to be there on the courthouse steps to meet them.

Battling Back:
A New Weapon in the War

In many ways, the Radical Left's long-standing practice of using time-consuming, expensive, intimidating, harassing lawsuits to get what it wants could be compared to the Iraqis' use of Scud missiles during Operation Desert Storm.

They launch one, hoping it will hit its mark, but even if it doesn't, maybe it will do enough damage to bludgeon the opponents into surrendering.

The difference is that it is a weapon that the Left has used with frightening success.

Time after time, in cities and towns all across America, groups like the ACLU have used such lawsuits to force their own twisted view of "civil rights" or "voting rights" on localities which don't see things the same way they do.

And when you represent a small municipality already deeply involved in financial difficulties, the thought of fighting prolonged litigation is something you can't bear.

So you give in, surrender, agree to do whatever it is the ultraliberals want you to do, whether it's right or wrong.

If you fight the case and lose, not only will you have to do what they want, but in their time-honored tradition, they'll also see that you get hit hard to pay the costs and attorneys fees they incurred in breaking your back.

And if you fight and win, you've spent a ton of money to keep the status quo that your constituents elected you to do—and you may have bankrupted your locality in the process.

One of those arguing for a strong reform of the system is WLF's Chief Counsel, Richard Samp.

> *We need a strong deterrent against baseless lawsuits if we are ever to bring under control the crisis in our court system. The litigation explosion that has occurred in this country over the past two decades is threatening to undermine our system of justice. It happens all too often that mainstream Americans are hit with frivolous lawsuits; if they choose to fight and eventually win, often their only reward is a hefty legal bill from their own attorney.*

There's been no other choice. Until recently.

Several major court decisions in which WLF has been involved hold out the hope that mainstream, honest Americans may have found their equivalent of a Patriot Missile with which to shoot down these Scuds in the form of something called Rule 11.

Actually, it's Rule 11 of the Federal Rules of Civil Procedure, which among other provisions, calls for sanctions if a lawsuit is filed "for any improper purpose, such as to harass or to cause unnecessary delay or needless increase in the cost of litigation."

Rule 11 was added to the Federal Rules of Civil Procedure in 1983 in an effort to slow or stem the raging tide of litigation in America's courts.

But it has only been in the past couple of years that the impact of Rule 11 has been felt.

Muzzling Kunstler

Perhaps no single individual more clearly represents the opposite of everything the Washington Legal Foundation stands for than William Kunstler. Certainly no single individual, from the days of his "defense" of the Chicago Seven, has abused the American judicial system, and the American people, more than he has.

A wild-eyed, long-haired radical, he has a very simple goal. He wants to destroy America. He's even admitted it, saying, "I am a double agent, working within the system to destroy the system."

That's his goal and what he has been working toward for more than two decades. Justice? The Constitution? Mere tools that the "system" provides for him to wrap himself protectively in while he works to destroy that same system.

But even Kunstler has now felt the sting of Rule 11.

He and two of his ultraliberal legal cronies were slapped by a courageous judge in North Carolina with fines of $123,000!

Judge Malcolm Howard of the U.S. District Court for the Eastern District of North Carolina, ruled that the lawyers violated Rule 11 by filing a lawsuit for an "improper purpose," and which was not "well grounded in fact and warranted by existing law."

WLF General Counsel Dan Popeo reacted to Judge Howard's decision with great delight, adding that the Judge's description of the lawsuit in question "fits almost every one of the lawsuits filed by the likes of Kunstler, the ACLU, the NAACP Legal Defense Fund, People for the American Way, and every other Radical Left legal group for the past 25 years."

The circumstances that led Judge Howard to his decision are these:

Two men, Eddie Hatcher and Timothy Jacobs, staged an armed takeover of a Robeson County, North Carolina newspaper office to protest alleged abuses by local law enforcement officials.

The men were charged in state court with kidnapping. But Kunstler, joined by an attorney from the ultraliberal Christic Institute and another from the University of North Carolina School of Law, filed suit in federal court to try and get around the state-court prosecution.

Kunstler's federal case charged North Carolina Governor James G. Martin and Attorney General Lacy B. Thornburg with conspiracy to deprive Hatcher and Jacobs of their First Amendment rights to free speech!

(Dan Popeo noted that, "as usual, Kunstler has a different copy of the Constitution than I do. Nowhere in mine does it say that armed kidnapping is a fundamental right protected by the First Amendment.")

In this case, however, the "defendants" decided to fight back against Kunstler's bullying tactic. They filed a motion to have the ridiculous federal lawsuit dismissed.

When Kunstler and his cronies realized their targets weren't going to back down this time, they reacted as all bullies do. They immediately withdrew their lawsuit in a great, "hey, just kidding folks" manner.

But the North Carolina officials who had been the targets of these radicals decided this time not to let them off even that easy.

Citing Rule 11, which permits a federal judge to

order anyone who makes a frivolous court filing to pay the legal fees of the opposing party, the state asked for reimbursement of its legal fees.

Judge Howard agreed. He ordered the three attorneys to reimburse $83,000 in defense costs. Then he imposed an additional sanction on each attorney of $10,000 "because of the egregious nature of the violations of Rule 11 in the present case."

The judge said that the Kunstler lawsuit was filed "for publicity, to embarrass state and county officials, to use as leverage in criminal proceedings, to obtain discovery for use in criminal proceedings, and to intimidate."

Screaming like stuck pigs, Kunstler and his radical allies immediately filed an appeal.

And no one was the least bit surprised when they were joined in that appeal by such other activist groups as the ACLU, the North Carolina Association of Black Lawyers, and the North Carolina Chapter of the National Lawyers Guild.

Nor was anyone surprised when WLF entered the case, representing among others, U.S. Senator Jesse Helms and U.S. Representatives Howard Coble and J. Alex McMillan.

In the fall of 1990, the U.S. Court of Appeals for the Fourth Circuit in Richmond, Virginia, agreed with WLF and upheld the sanctions against Kunstler and his cronies.

It was then, according to Dan Popeo, that America got the best news of all. Here's how he told the story:

The best news of all was what he [Kunstler] said after the appeals court decision. Let me quote him exactly so there's no doubt.

> *"I'll tell you this,"* Kunstler said, *"I'm not going to pay any fine. I'm going to rot in jail if that's what I have to do to dramatize this thing."*
>
> Then he added, *"I think I could do no better thing for my country."*
>
> He's right. For once William Kunstler and I agree on something: there is no better thing he could do for America than rot in jail.

Of course, before he would rot in jail, Kunstler had to try to get the Supreme Court to hear his case. So he filed a Petition for Writ of Certiorari to ask the court to do that.

If the involvement at the Appeals Court level was intense, it was nothing compared to the cast of characters that came out of the woodwork to take Kunstler's side in trying to persuade the Supreme Court.

Among those players were Ralph Nader's Public Citizen Litigation Group; all sorts of attorneys, including some of the most visible and active of the Radical Left; and an array of other groups that included the National Council of Churches of Christ, the Southern Christian Leadership Conference, the Southern Organizing Committee for Economic and Social Justice, the Center for Democratic Renewal, Clergy and Laity Concerned, the Federation of Southern Cooperatives/Land Assistance Fund, the Gulf Coast Tenant Organization, Highlander Research and Education Center, Institution for Southern Studies, North Carolinians against Racist and Religious Violence, the People's Institute for Survival and Beyond, the Southern Rainbow Education Fund, and the Southeast Center for Justice.

Kunstler's team used two primary arguments to try and convince the Supreme Court to hear the case.

First, they contended that the district court lost its power to impose Rule 11 sanctions once the underlying lawsuit had been dismissed.

Second, they contended that the district court denied them their right to an evidentiary hearing at which they could have contested claims that their lawsuit was frivolous.

In urging the Supreme Court not to hear the case, WLF attorneys argued that both those arguments lacked merit. The Foundation noted that the attorneys had numerous opportunities to refute the charges against them—through written briefs, affidavits of key witnesses, and oral arguments before the district court.

WLF also argued that to require evidentiary hearings (i.e., hearings at which witnesses testify and are then subject to cross-examination) in all Rule 11 proceedings would emasculate Rule 11 by raising the costs of such proceedings to such a height that victims of Rule 11 violations could not afford to press their claims.

On April 15, 1991, the U.S. Supreme Court denied Kunstler a Writ of Certiorari, refusing to hear the case.

That action means the determination that this radical violated Rule 11 can no longer be challenged, and the only housekeeping remaining is for the district court in North Carolina to determine the exact and final amount of the Rule 11 sanction. . . . (And for Dan Popeo to see if there's any way he can help Kunstler get his wish of rotting in jail.)

Already Hit Other Targets, too

Just as William Kunstler is by no means the only Radical who has used intimidating lawsuits in an effort to gain in the courtroom what he can't hope to win in the voting booth, neither is he the only target hit so far by Rule 11.

Almost as satisfying as a direct hit on Kunstler is one on Ramsey Clark. This man, who was once, as Lyndon Johnson's Attorney General, America's highest ranking law enforcement officer, seems to have devoted his life to attacking the country he once took an oath to defend.

The more radical the cause, the more anti-American the characters involved, the more likely Clark is to be involved.

As is seen elsewhere in this book, he even showed up in Baghdad during the height of Operation Desert Storm, glaring out at the world from CNN's cameras, yammering away about American atrocities!

Well, Clark too has been hit with Rule 11 sanctions, ordered to pick up defense costs for the ridiculous lawsuit he brought against the United States and President Reagan in particular.

That was the case, also included elsewhere in this book, where he brought suit on behalf of some of Moammar Khadafy's Libyans, seeking damages because of the surgical bombing strike Reagan ordered against the Mad Dog of Libya.

Another Rule 11 case in which WLF was involved was *Cooter & Gell v. Hartmarx*.

In this case, a law firm filed an antitrust suit on

behalf of its corporate client against a competing company.

The suit was filed without proper research, and the plaintiff's factual assumptions turned out to be untrue.

As a result, the federal judge who heard the case used Rule 11 to impose monetary sanctions on the attorneys who filed the suit.

Again, WLF argued in its Supreme Court brief that a court may impose Rule 11 sanctions on an attorney even if he withdraws his suit before the defendant has filed an answer.

The Supreme Court agreed with that position and upheld the sanctions.

Only by preventing such harassing, frivolous lawsuits from ever being brought in the first place will America ever recover its court system from the control of the Radical Left.

Rule 11 could go a long way in helping make that possible.

WASHINGTON LEGAL FOUNDATION

Daniel J. Popeo
General Counsel and President

Constance Claffey Larcher
Executive Director

Paul D. Kamenar
Executive Legal Director

Richard A. Samp
Chief Counsel

John C. Scully
Counsel

Alan M. Slobodin
President and General Counsel
Legal Studies Division

Christopher A. Sterbenz
Executive Legal Director
Legal Studies Division

BOARD OF ADVISORS

Honorable John Ashcroft
Governor of Missouri

Honorable Robert E. Badham
Former U.S. Representative

Honorable Norman H. Bangerter
Governor of Utah

Honorable Joe Barton
U.S. Representative

Honorable Herbert A. Bateman
U.S. Representative

Honorable Helen Delich Bentley
U.S. Representative

Honorable John Boehner
U.S. Representative

Honorable Beau Boulter
Former U.S. Representative

William Bowen, President
Garvon, Inc.

Honorable Jim Bunning
U.S. Representative

Honorable Dave Camp
U.S. Representative

Honorable Carroll A. Campbell, Jr.
Governor of South Carolina

Honorable Tim Lee Carter
Former U.S. Representative

Honorable William F. Clinger, Jr.
U.S. Representative

Joseph Coors
Adolph Coors Company

Honorable Christopher Cox
U.S. Representative

Honorable Philip M. Crane
U.S. Representative

Honorable William E. Dannemeyer
U.S. Representative

Honorable Jack Davis
Former U.S. Representative

Honorable Tom DeLay
U.S. Representative

Honorable Jeremiah Denton, Jr.
Former U.S. Senator

Honorable Michael DeWine
Lt. Governor of Ohio

Honorable William L. Dickinson
U.S. Representative

Honorable Joseph J. DioGuardi
Former U.S. Representative

Honorable Robert K. Dornan
U.S. Representative

Honorable David T. Dreier
U.S. Representative

Honorable Mickey Edwards
U.S. Representative

Honorable Bill Emerson
U.S. Representative

Rawles Fulgham
Merrill Lynch Private Capital, Inc.

Lt. Gen. Daniel Graham, USA, Ret.
Director, High Frontier

Honorable Charles Grassley
U.S. Senator

Honorable John Paul Hammerschmidt
U.S. Representative

Honorable J. Dennis Hastert
U.S. Representative

Honorable Larry E. Craig
U.S. Senator

Honorable Orrin Hatch
U.S. Senator

Honorable Jesse Helms
U.S. Senator

Honorable Paul B. Henry
U.S. Representative

Peter D. Herder, President
Herder Companies

E. T. Hermann, President
Pacific Freeport Warehouse Co.

Honorable Larry J. Hopkins
U.S. Representative

Honorable Gordon Humphrey
N.H. State Senator

Honorable Henry J. Hyde
U.S. Representative

Fred G. Karem, Esq.
Lexington, KY

Honorable John R. Kasich
U.S. Representative

Honorable Thomas Kindness
Former U.S. Representative

Honorable Robert J. Lagomarsino
U.S. Representative

Honorable Jerry Lewis
U.S. Representative

James R. Lightner, Ret. Chairman
Electrospace Systems

Honorable Bob Livingston
U.S. Representative

Honorable Dan Lungren
California Attorney General

Honorable James McClure
Former U.S. Senator

Honorable Bill McCollum
U.S. Representative

Honorable Bob McEwen
U.S. Representative

Honorable John Miller
U.S. Representative

Honorable Carlos J. Moorhead
U.S. Representative

Bill Murchison, Editor
Dallas Morning News

Honorable Michael G. Oxley
U.S. Representative

Honorable Ron Packard
U.S. Representative

Honorable Thomas E. Petri
U.S. Representative

Honorable John Edward Porter
U.S. Representative

Honorable Donald L. Ritter
U.S. Representative

George Roche, President
Hillsdale College

Honorable William V. Roth, Jr.
U.S. Senator

Honorable Eldon Rudd
Former U.S. Representative

Honorable Dan Schaefer
U.S. Representative

Herbert Schiff, President
H.G. Schiff & Company

Honorable William D. Schuette
Former U.S. Representative

Robert Shortley, President
National Public Affairs

Honorable Norman Shumway
Former U.S. Representative

Roy W. Simmons, Chairman
Zion First National Bank

Clyde Sluhan, President
Master Chemical Corp.

Honorable Gerald B. Solomon
U.S. Representative

Honorable Floyd D. Spence
U.S. Representative

Honorable Steven D. Symms
U.S. Senator

Honorable Barbara Vucanovich
U.S. Representative

Honorable Robert Walker
U.S. Representative

Richard S. Williamson, Esq.
Mayer, Brown and Platt

Honorable Frank R. Wolf
U.S. Representative

Robert Woodson, President
National Center for Neighborhood Enterprise

Honorable George Wortley
Former U.S. Representative

About the Washington Legal Foundation

The Washington Legal Foundation was founded in 1977 by Daniel J. Popeo as a nonpartisan, public interest law institution organized to engage in litigation and the administrative process in matters affecting the broad public interest.

An independent nationwide corporation not associated or affiliated with any other organization, the Foundation devotes a substantial portion of its resources to defending individual rights, aiding victims of violent crimes, challenging regulations which impede a free market economy, and supporting a strong national defense.

Its ability to litigate high profile landmark legal cases is unmatched and has proven to be an invaluable resource: WLF has represented some 200 Senators and Representatives as well as business and civic groups and hardworking taxpayers in courtrooms all across the country.

Its Legal Studies Division defends the legal, political and economic ideals embodied in the Constitution and works to discover, develop and promote the intellectual legal defenders of our free market system. Even more important, this Division is an effective counter against the radical young professors who are teaching students that the American legal system is primarily an instrument of social, economic and political oppression by the ruling political and business elite.

By combining its litigation activities and its legal

policy efforts, WLF has firmly established itself as a legal catalyst for responsible judicial reform.

The Foundation is classified as a Section 501 (c) (3) organization under the Internal Revenue Code of 1954. Individuals, corporations, companies, associations and foundations are eligible to support the work of the Foundation through tax-deductible gifts.

Background material will be provided to substantiate WLF's tax-deductibility.

Use the coupon below to send your tax-deductible contribution to support the work of the Washington Legal Foundation as America's voice in the courts.

☐ YES! As an honest, mainstream American, I am glad to finally have a voice in my nation's courts. To help make that voice even stronger, I am proud to send my tax-deductible contribution of:

☐ $_____   ☐ $1,000   ☐ $500

☐ $100   ☐ $50   ☐ $25   ☐ $15

Please make check payable to: Washington Legal Foundation

Name_____

Address_____

City/State/Zip_____

☐ Please send me more information about WLF, America's Voice in the Courts.

Washington Legal Foundation
1705 N Street, N.W.
Washington, D.C. 20036

"Until WLF, 'public interest' seemed to be synonymous with the term 'liberal.'

Groups like the ACLU, like Ralph Nader's Public Citizen group, like William Kunstler's Center for Constitutional Rights, had exerted enormous influence over America's court system and were the darlings of the news media.

WLF has changed all that."

**From the Foreword by
U.S. Senator Orrin Hatch**

Changed all that and more! Here is a close-up look at the most productive and effective pro-free enterprise public interest law firm in America, the Washington Legal Foundation.

From fighting in America's war on drugs to demanding rights for the victims of violent crimes, from blowing the whistle on ultralenient or incompetent judges to going toe-to-toe with the American Bar Association, the Washington Legal Foundation has finally given mainstream, honest Americans a voice in the courts.

A powerful voice.